FROM THE RIVER
TO THE SEA

T0078348

FROM THE RIVER TO THE SEA

A LIFE'S JOURNEY FROM INDIA TO SOUTH AMERICA

Joseph Matchanickal

PARTRIDGE

A Penguin Company

Partridge books may be ordered through booksellers or by contacting:

Partridge India
Penguin Books India Pvt.Ltd
11, Community Centre, Panchsheel Park, New Delhi 110017
India
www.partridgepublishing.com
Phone: 000.800.10062.62

CONTENTS

DEDICATION

To my mother, who bore and loved me to the core of her heart. She was like a tiger that fed and sheltered her cubs—ten of them. She never blinked for one second from her duty. Thanks to her, all her cubs are grown and have their own families. She is in heaven enjoying her reward.

To the Blessed Mother of Guadalupe in Mexico City. She appeared more than five hundred years ago to a native Indian and her shrine is the most visited pilgrim spot in the world.

To Mother Teresa of Calcutta and her Sisters of Charity for inspiring me to lead a better life.

ACKNOWLEDGEMENTS

My sincere thanks to Savita John, my friend who lived in Venezuela, for her patience to read through the manuscript and correcting it. Without her help, this work would not have been possible.

To my children and my wife for suggesting various changes which have been incorporated. Thank you for your encouragement, love and support throughout the years.

PREFACE

At twenty-nine, I ventured outside my tiny village in Kerala, India into the world, a journey that took me forty years to complete. How did I start this journey? One day in 1969, I walked out of the US Consulate in Madras with my heartbeat still racing and my palms feeling sticky from the sweat. I had just proposed to the Fulbright committee my subject of study: Science Education, which seems like a fairly straightforward task had it not been for the fact that I had come up with that idea just 5 minutes before standing in front of the committee. The result? Anxious months of waiting with a faint hope that luck would be on my side and finally a letter announcing I had been approved for a scholarship to study in the US. My life from then on changed forever . . .

Fast-forward 40 years and two of my granddaughters are anxiously waiting for me on Skype, they want "Buelo Joe" ("grandpa Joe") to tell them a story. We speak Spanish to each other as I do to my three kids who were born and brought up in Venezuela. I am tempted to tell my granddaughters the stories in this book but I hold back, maybe they will appreciate it more in a few years down the road. This book is for them. For now I tell them about the tiger and the elephant who meet in the forest, with sheer delight they listen on, and as the story twists and turns each of my words is met with eyes wide open, full of anticipation . . .

The stories above serve as bookends, but in between these pages you will read the rest of the journey. It takes the reader from Lansing, Michigan in the 1960's to the oil fields in Venezuela in the 1970's to Caracas in the 1980's to Curacao in the 1990's as well as a small town in the hills bordering Colombia. I moved the family seventeen times, crossed the Caribbean Sea more than a hundred times, I have seen seven presidents of Venezuela taking office, witnessed two military coups, two popular rebellions and thirty thousand people washed into the sea by a mudslide on the other side of the hill where I lived. I love that I have come to know Latin America and its people, can understand nuances in culture and I'm familiar with the slang. As a 73-year-old retired now living in Kerala, I identify with the five hundred million Spanish and Portuguese speaking folks and have enjoyed every bit of our stay among them. My wife and I raised three wonderful kids and now joyfully await pictures, news and Skype calls from our four granddaughters and our children. With a son in law from Guatemala, one from Kenya/Goa and a daughter in law from Venezuela I can truly say I would have never imagined that life would turn out this way for a young man from a humble village in Kerala. Life can be truly surprising for those who are willing to embark upon the journey. This book tries to tell that story.

Please note that this is not an autobiography; it is just a novel based on a real story line around my life. Some of the events, circumstances and descriptions are carefully altered to put in the pieces that hold the narration together. The core events are kept intact so that the final product has the flavor of the base fruit. I have used pseudonyms to protect the identity of persons in this story. I hope you will enjoy reading this book as much as I did in writing it and I hope you will find inspiration to foray into your own adventure.—The Author

CHAPTER ONE

In Search of a Destiny

Prior to leaving my house after the vacations, I noticed a piece of cloth with strong blood stains lying in the work area of the kitchen. I asked my mother about it, and she confided to me that she had been suffering from a bleeding problem for several years. She had exhausted all the medical help locally available from Ayurvedic doctors, and she wanted to see a doctor in a hospital. I took her to a doctor at the Calicut Medical College Hospital, several miles away. The doctor's prognosis was that she needed immediate surgery to remove the uterus. I had neither money nor holidays to spend for the immediate surgery. I brought her home and asked her to rest until I returned. I was going to request additional leave. If it was not given, I was prepared to resign. I believed my mother's health was the most important, over all other things in life. She was only fifty-two years old, full of life and, was most needed by all of us, especially by my last five younger brothers. She was the life of the family, and I did not have second thoughts about resigning from my job, if needed, to take care of her. I could not rely on the other able members of my family to look after her in the hospital. They were not educated and had no economic means to support her. If some complications arose, I wanted to be there to make the necessary decisions.

All through the journey in the train back to the school where I taught, I thought about the future of my brothers. I knew that the younger ones would drop out from school at some stage, get married and have children, live in thatched huts and make a meager living from the small piece of land which they would inherit from their parents. The married ones were already on their way to this inevitable end. Their peers smoked and had ended up as drunkards and wife-beaters. I wanted them to have a better life and, a different destiny. I believed that leaving our earlier home in Mid Kerala, where most of our family still lived, was a mistake. At least, in case of difficulties, there were relatives to turn to. The practice of dropping out from school was not encouraged by the close family or, for that matter, the society in Mid Kerala. In Northern Malabar, where we resided, dropping out of school was common because the parents needed the children to work in the land. I was convinced that education was the only way to liberate my younger brothers from the bondage of under-development and help them look for a better destiny. On that train, I vowed that I would ensure a good future for my brothers.

I applied for a month's leave, but the school authorities instead, requested my resignation. They had a Brother to replace me immediately. I tendered my resignation and the Brother took over my job. I stayed on until I could orient and train the Brother. One week after my arrival, I was on the train back to Calicut with two hundred and twelve rupees in the pocket. I took a room near the Calicut Medical College Hospital. My older brother arrived the next day with our mother. I got her admitted into the Hospital, visited the doctor at his home, and paid him fifty rupees to take extra care of her, as was customary to ensure that the patient got better attention. Since it was a government hospital, the costs associated with the treatment and stay, were free. The surgery went off well, but the doctor informed me that she was in pretty bad shape, and that she was one step away from developing uterine cancer. While my mother convalesced, I took time out to hunt for a job. All my relatives who came to visit my mother discouraged me from looking for a job in Kerala. They warned me that all teaching positions in private schools and colleges were obtained on the basis of bribes metered out as donations. Positions in public institutions were given on the basis of party affiliations. I neither had the money for donations nor the party affiliation in order to qualify for a job. I did not even know any important person to recommend me for a post. Nevertheless, I applied to two colleges for a position as Lecturer of Chemistry. I received interview calls from the principals of both colleges. They were quick to notice my good grades. I thought that both principals were impressed by my command of English and my verbal capacity. I left the interviews, feeling optimistic, but I was told by my relatives that the interviews were a mere formality to appoint pre-selected candidates of their own choice. I refused to accept this conclusion for lack of evidence. I had the conviction, or may-be the illusion, that my destiny was in my own hands, and that I could bend any situation to my advantage. For the time being, I remained confident that I had done my part, and God would do the rest.

My mother was released five days after her surgery, and I took her home to recuperate. When I arrived home, there were two telegrams waiting for me from the colleges where I had been interviewed. Both said that I had been selected to teach Chemistry in their respective colleges. I could not believe it and couldn't have been happier. I gave thanks to God for making it happen. My family was very happy. At last, they saw some light at the end of the tunnel to their economic woes. I selected the college where I wanted to teach. However, I sent a telegram to the principal of the other college which I did not select. In it, I thanked him for the offer and excused myself for not accepting it. However, I had to join the college I selected in two days. This meant I had to return to Calicut the very next day. After spending the evening with several visitors who came to enquire about our mother's health, I was unable to fall asleep due to excitement. The next morning, I left for Calicut and reported for work. I was assigned twelve hours of teaching per week. I did not have to prepare much, because I knew the subject well. I took a room in the college hostel meant for staff and dined in the college restaurant. I was paid a handsome sum of five hundred and thirty two rupees per month, a substantial increase from my salary as a school teacher. Of course, in my previous job I didn't have to pay for boarding and lodging. I enjoyed the teaching experience and had enough time to relax. I went around the town during the weekends with colleagues and friends and watched many movies that I had missed.

In the meantime, my cousin Lissy got married to a gentleman whom I lovingly called Alian. He held two part time jobs, one as a journalist and the other as an insurance agent. Lissy and Alian lived in the same town where I taught. One day, Alian and Lissy suggested that we jointly rent a house to share and cut costs. Lissy was a graduate nurse. I liked the idea, and so we moved into a house and hired a lady to cook, clean, and take care of the house. One of my younger brothers called Mohan, whom I got admitted into a boarding facility for students from low income families, passed his high school exams and moved in with us. I taught him Mathematics, Physics and Chemistry so that he could take the entrance exam for the Aeronautical Technician course in the Indian Navy. Six months into the preparation, Mohan took the exam and passed. He also appeared for the interview in Bombay and was selected for the three years Diploma Course for Aircraft Maintenance.

I really wished to go to the US for work or study, to escape from my life of limited economic prospects in India. I wanted to help my parents in a real way, plus educate my five younger brothers who were at the school level. Also, I had to settle down the four brothers who had quit their studies. By this time, three of them were married with children. One day, in the barber's shop, I saw a sports magazine from the US, in which there was an advertisement for car salesmen; the address of the Head of Sales was also there. I wrote him a long letter, explaining my precarious lot in India and requesting sponsorship from him to go to the US to work for him. The request letter was long, and it took me a few hours to compose. I never got a reply. I would never know if the guy ever got the letter. I was disappointed for the lack of reply and even felt stupid for having written in the first place. Such was my despair that I behaved irrationally. In any case, I believed I had let my Creator know my need. I was sure that I would get an answer in due time.

One day, one of Alian's friends came to our house and informed us that this friend's brother had been admitted to the Calicut Medical College Hospital for snake bite. This friend was Alian's neighbor in the hills where his parents lived. I went to the hospital after classes to see the patient, for I had never met anybody bitten by a snake before. What I saw impacted me forever. The patient was rolling, shivering from pain, and sweating blood. One of the nurses told me that the condition of the person was very delicate. She said that if somebody donated blood, it was possible for the patient to survive. I offered to donate blood, and the nurse drew two liters of blood from me. As I returned to the bedside of the patient, he was breathing his last. I felt disappointed, even cheated; this was the first time I had donated blood to save somebody. I consoled myself that somebody else would benefit from my donation.

I received news from home that my father had again disappeared. I imagined the debts he would have left behind. I went home to console my mother and support my brothers. I paid off the debts. I also took the time to go to the school where my younger brothers studied and enquired about their performance. All of them needed more concentration into their studies. They needed the discipline of a boarding. The next week, taking leave from the college, I did some quick visits to locate boarding schools where my brothers could study. I could not find any that fit my budget, but found an orphanage quite far away. My brothers were not qualified to be admitted there, as they were not orphans. I explained to the priest in charge that they were practically orphans, as their father was absent from the family most of the time. Yes, I had stretched the truth a little bit. The priest listened carefully and read my face with penetrating looks. He wanted to know if I was telling the truth, or if I was an imposter who wanted to take undue advantage of the free boarding, lodging and education reserved for orphans. After carefully weighing my story, he decided to admit three of my younger brothers into his institution and requested me to send whatever donations I could afford out of my salary. I promised to do so and left the place after thanking him sincerely. After one week, I was back-with my brothers and left them there under the care of the priest. Another brother was left at home to continue studies in the local school. I asked one of the local teachers to follow up on his studies closely. To be fair to my brothers, I have to note that they all improved in their studies, especially in the college, and have turned out to be excellent professionals, all pursuing the American dream.

One day, I saw an advertisement in the Indian Express, calling for applications for the Fulbright Scholarship program from qualified candidates from different specializations with research experience, preferably with published papers, for postgraduate studies in the US. Chemistry was one of the subjects where scholarships were available. I did not care about the advertisement, thinking that my one year of experience in high school teaching was very limited to qualify for the scholarship. I knew my chances for a scholarship in Chemistry were none, given the likelihood that I was to compete among people with research experience and published papers in professional journals. My two degrees in chemistry from prestigious colleges and my grades were impressive; however, my two years of experience was limited to high school teaching. The cutting from the Indian Express stayed in the waste-paper basket for several days, since the housekeeper had not come for work, as she was sick. Every time I saw the advertisement, I felt disappointed that I was not qualified enough to apply for the scholarship. Alian, too, saw the advertisement in another city on his journalistic travels, and he cut out the advertisement and kept it safe. When he returned, he asked me if I had seen the advertisement, and I told him that I had thrown it away into the trash. Alian scolded me for having done so without consulting him. I searched the trash basket, but the lady had already burnt the trash. Alian then pulled out the advertisement from his bag and asked me to apply. He said that if nothing came out of it, I would have lost only the postage. I sent for an application form, which duly arrived, and I filled in the information, included copies of all the required documents, and mailed the packet. I was very sure that I would never hear from the Fulbright Foundation.

A month later, much to my surprise, I got instructions in the mail from the Fulbright Foundation to appear for an interview at the American Consulate in Madras, and to take with me the originals of all the supporting documents. I reported on the specified day and hour at the consulate. The consulate was full of people being interviewed for the Scholarship. Initially, I stood, as there was no place to sit. As people started going in, chairs became available. I quietly sat down in one of them and patiently awaited my turn. I overheard two people discussing their careers after their Masters in Chemistry. One of them was engaged in research in a prestigious institution in Bangalore. The other was working in the Research and Development Division of a well-known tanning company in Madras. Both had published papers in professional journals. I found out the interviews were being conducted for graduates of Chemistry that day, and they were from all the four states of South India. The US Consulate was playing the role of the screening body for the selection of the Fulbright Scholarship grantees. I felt as if I had no business to be there at all. I felt very small amongst those people who were exhibiting and gloating over credentials much better than mine. This was the moment when pessimism got the better of me. However, as fast as I sank, I quickly sprang up, and took stock of my strengths and competitive advantages. I thought I could speak better English than several of them, at least the ones I overheard. Then, I sank again, not knowing what I would propose to study during the interview; I stood no chance to be awarded a scholarship to study chemistry. What else would I propose to study if it was not Chemistry? The time was approaching for my interview, and I had no clue. I had to propose something different, which would be of interest for the interviewers. I felt like walking away, as my mind was blank. If I stayed for the interview, I had to come up with something quick. I began to sweat and got desperate, not knowing what to do, to stay or walk away. I was afraid that I would end up as a lecturer for the rest of my life, which in itself was not a bad profession; but, I wanted to go to the US and study further to have a better future. Suddenly, it occurred to me, to propose to study how to teach science to high school students. It must have been an inspiration from God. Then my name was called out for the interview. I did not have sufficient time to mature my thoughts before I found myself in front of the committee.

The committee consisted of three people; all of them were professors of different colleges in Madras City. I immediately recognized one of them as Professor Prasad, who was my Chemistry professor at Loyola College, and whom I had not seen for three years. Professor Prasad did not recognize me immediately. The Committee welcomed me for the interview and asked me to sit down. They went through the originals of my credentials. I was trembling, for I was afraid they would kick me forthright for lack of sufficient and proper experience. They asked me a few basic questions in Chemistry, and I answered them all. They started asking me some general questions about India, and I answered most of them correctly. They changed their questions to general information of the world, and I felt comfortable in answering them, as I had cultivated the habit of reading. Those readings stood me in good stead. Then they asked me what I wanted to study in the US. At this point, professor Prasad asked me if I had studied at Loyola College, to which I replied in the affirmative. I told the Committee that I wanted to study under the Fulbright Program how to teach science to high school students. I explained all that I knew and imagined about the subject. I titled my subject of study as Science Education. One of the professors asked me, "What is Science Education?" Before I could answer, Professor Prasad intervened and explained to the rest of the members what Science Education was, thus sparing me the embarrassment of explaining what I was not sure about. Professor Prasad understood what I was proposing, for he was a member of The National Council for Educational Research in Teaching (NCERT) in Delhi, a well-known institution in India for the promotion of Science Education. Professor Prasad asked me if I had heard about NCERT and I explained well what the institution stood for. Professor Prasad was impressed, but told me that the Fulbright Program did not offer its scholarship in this field. He told me that the Committee could not recommend me for studies in Chemistry, for there were more qualified aspirants. They apologized for having to send me away empty-handed. I picked up my papers, thanked them for the interview, and left the room, dejected and totally lost. I was perspiring profusely. I sat on the bench outside to catch my breath. I consoled myself, saying that not everything was lost, that I still had a job. I did not hear them calling for the next person. I was about to pick up my bag and walk away when I heard my name being called out again, asking me to go in yet again. I went in still sweating from the blow I had received. Professor Prasad told me that the committee was pleased with my interview, but was sorry that the Fulbright Scholarship Program did not consider grants to study Science Education. Nevertheless, Professor Prasad continued, the Selection Committee would forward my application to the Grants Committee in New Delhi to be processed. They said that if there was any possibility, I would hear from New Delhi. I was happy that there was at least a ray of hope. I thanked them again for the special consideration and left the room. I sat down again on the same bench and pondered over what was happening to me. It had been one hell of a roller coaster ride! I concluded that my trip to Madras was not a total loss after all. The comment of one of my colleagues haunted me at this time; he had told me that I would have a hard time in the world for being short in stature. I believed it and felt bad for it too; worse still, I couldn't do anything about it. I sat down for a while on that bench and consoled myself that the colleague was wrong, that height had nothing to do with opportunities in life, with the exception of the military, civil aviation, or sports. I felt I had advanced a little bit in life. I picked up my bag and left the place. I went and ate a good lunch, and by evening I boarded the train back to Calicut.

I explained to Alian and Lissy all that had happened at the Consulate. They encouraged me to keep my hopes high. Back at work, I was appointed as the Examiner for Chemistry for Kerala University in the final exams. I was to supervise the practical exams in two colleges. Meanwhile, I received a letter from the Fulbright Scholarship Foundation in Delhi, informing me that my application had been forwarded to the International Institute of Education (IIE) in New York, to look for possible scholarship opportunities in American universities. The IIE is the official administrator of the Fulbright Scholarships Program worldwide. I was happy that I had passed the Delhi hurdle too. I crossed my fingers and waited. As I was conducting the exams in one of the colleges, Alian called me to inform that there was a telegram from IIE informing that I had been admitted to the University of Wisconsin in Milwaukee, and that the university offered me the Stickney Scholarship to finance my studies. The next day, Alian brought me the telegram, which confirmed what he told over the telephone. However, there was a condition. I had to carry 1200 US Dollars from my own funds to meet my living expenses, and I had to be prepared to travel to the US within sixty days from New Delhi. Again, I felt I was thrown to the middle of an ocean with high winds from all directions. One thousand two hundred dollars translated into approximately ten thousand rupees, and I had hardly three hundred rupees in my possession. This was no small sum for a poor church mouse like me. Where would I get such a large sum of money? My parents wouldn't have been able to raise this money, even if they sold all their property. They even owed money on their property to educate me in college. Even if I got the money, how would I wind up the exams, correct five hundred papers, and get all the documents ready from the scratch within sixty days? A new passport alone took more than forty-five days. Then, I had to prepare and write the Test of English as a Foreign Language (TOEFL), obtain acceptable scores and forward the results to the University. I had to change rupees into dollars, for which I had to get permission from Reserve Bank of India, a government institution that took its own time to approve such applications. Finally, I would have to go back to the American Consulate in Madras to get a visa to the US. If everything went well, I would board the plane to Delhi from Coimbatore on 10th of July for one day of orientation in NCERT, and then fly to New York on the 12th. The challenge seemed insurmountable. I was so close to realizing my dream, and yet so many hurdles to be crossed. There was a brief moment when I thought that it would have been better if I had not been selected so that I could have avoided this agony. I was dejected and almost gave up, but the fighter in me took control and charged me to muster all my energy and intelligence to achieve the goal. On a piece of paper, I listed out the actions I had to complete and put a time frame for each action. It was as if I had to cut my way through the forest and swim the rivers to reach the other side in a limited time.

My first priority was to finish the exams, correct the papers and send the scores to the university. In the first college, a girl and her father came to plead me to be lenient in correcting her papers. I did not consider the petition at all, as I was bothered that they came to my room in the hotel and asked for the favor without shame. In the second college, a boy helped a girl copy from his papers. I expelled both of them from the exams. They were allowed back, as the principal of the college intervened and made the two students apologize. I buried myself in a hotel for a week to correct the papers and mail the results to the university. Something very curious happened the last day at the hotel. A woman knocked on my door and asked me for a lime. I said I did not have any, and I saw her knocking on other doors without success. I felt bad that she needed a lime very badly and that people in the other rooms also sent her away empty-handed. I went out and bought some limes, looked for her and handed them over to her.

She looked at me strangely and walked away with the lime. It is only after I left the hotel that it occurred to me that she had different intentions, and that the lime was just an excuse for contacting clients. I mentioned this incident to a friend and he told me a story. He found his cousin with a bruise on the head. He asked him, "What happened?" The cousin explained, "I hit my head with the hammer I had in my hand, when I thought of a lady that knocked on my room for a lime and how stupid I was to send her away".

I had to take several simultaneous actions, but the most important one was to get somebody to loan me ten thousand rupees so that I could buy the one thousand two hundred US dollars. Initially, I was lost as to what I would do. I approached the father of a boy I had taught in the high school; this person was a well known business-man who turned me down without giving any explanation. Alian asked me to approach the Bishop of Calicut, who was Italian. Alian's argument was that, being a foreigner, the Bishop would be more empathetic to my case than the local clergy. I had never met him before and found it very difficult to ask such a big sum of money from a stranger, even though he was a Bishop of the Catholic Church. Having been cornered without any other solution, I mustered the courage and knocked on the door of the Bishop, and he welcomed me with a warm smile. Here was an old man, probably in his early eighties. I kissed his ring and accommodated myself on the chair he tendered. I identified myself as a professor of the nearby college and then proceeded to explain to him my predicament. The bishop listened carefully and empathetically. He asked me a couple of questions regarding the Fulbright Scholarship Program and the type of study I was planning to do in the US. He called his treasurer, who was a priest, and, without much ado, asked him to accompany me to the bank and transfer ten thousand rupees to my account. The priest made a gesture of obeisance. I did not expect him to make the decision that fast. I was touched by this profuse gesture of generosity. I had hardly spent half an hour with the bishop before he threw open his purse. I thanked him and bid goodbye to him by touching his feet. The bishop was touched by my gesture of gratitude. I accompanied the treasurer to the bank. I had to open an account first, in order to get the money transferred into my account. It was the first time that I was opening an account in a bank. The whole procedure took an hour. Two hours after I walked into the bishop's house, I was a different man. I felt that a heavy stone, under which I felt crushed, had been rolled away. I wanted to fly in the air and tell everyone about the miracle that had just happened. I had walked into the house of a stranger and walked out with a large sum of money, without guarantee and full of love. I felt that I had just visited God the Father Himself. The bishop's long white beard and physical stature supported this feeling in me. His name was Patroni, and he was well respected and loved by the town authorities and his faithful flock.

Nobody believed the feat I had pulled off. Everybody asked me how I had done it. I could only say that the hand of God was on me. I claimed that God had used the hands of the bishop to bless me with the money I needed. Alian and Lissy were surprised at the immediate response of the bishop, and were happy that I got the timely help from such an unexpected source.

My parents and siblings were very proud of me and announced the good news from the roof-top. With the major hurdle crossed, I still had many more chores to get done before I could cry victory. I still had to get a passport, take the TOEFL exam, get approval from the Reserve Bank of India to convert the rupees into dollars, get the US visa, and bid goodbye to my relatives. The travel plans had been arranged by and paid for by the IIE in New York. I applied for the passport, and the officer said it would take thirty to forty five days. I greased his palms a little bit, and he promised to speed up the process. I took the TOEFL test, scored well, and sent the results to the university. My bank applied to the Reserve Bank for the required permit to buy the dollars, and the permission was granted without delay. Once the passport was in my possession, I went back to the US Consulate in Madras for the student visa, which was issued the very next day. I resigned from the college after working only for a year. My mother quietly advised me not go to the US, leaving such a good job, which paid a decent salary with which the whole family could adjust to live. On prodding her a little further, I found out she was afraid that I would get married to somebody in the US without the involvement of parents. If that had happened, she was afraid that I would no longer be able to support the family economically. I assured her that I would never marry without her blessings. The tickets arrived and finally I got ready to begin the journey. I went around bidding goodbye to my relatives and friends. I visited Leela, my former girl-friend and neighbor, to bid goodbye. I found her with a two years old baby girl and expecting another child. She told me that her husband was diagnosed with cirrhosis. I did not know how to console her. A part of me was left there when I walked away from her. Somebody who was known to the family came around with a last-minute marriage proposal, which I turned down. As I was doing some last minute shopping in Calicut, I stumbled into my father, who had left the house for some time. Nobody knew where he was. He was passing through the town, but accepted to go with me to home after learning that I was about to travel to the US. I was careful to keep an eye on him all the time, so that he would not escape and run away again. We reached home, and my father became the usual silent person who had nothing to say. Nobody asked him any questions either. He quickly started working in the land fixing things. This was his way to escape from family people and local friends who came to inquire about him. He offered to stay home while everybody else accompanied me to the airport. I made a quick visit to the orphanage to bid goodbye to my younger brothers.

My itinerary was to fly from Coimbatore to Bangalore and from there to Delhi. Finally, after going through so much struggle and mental stress, I was on my way to the airport. Several of my uncles showed up at the airport, including Uncle Kurian, in spite of his advanced age and travel inconveniences. The final goodbye was tearful for all. My mother was full of tears and made me promise to be back after a year. She expressed her helplessness as to what she would do without me. Alian accompanied me in the flight up to Bangalore. When I reached Delhi, I did not know to which hotel I should go. I was in Delhi for the first time and didn't know anybody there. I asked a rickshaw driver to take me to an inexpensive hotel. The rickshaw driver ended up taking me to a hotel in Old Delhi through narrow and winding alleys. I checked into the hotel and looked for a restaurant to eat some food. It was past 10 pm on Sunday, and no restaurants were open nearby. I told another rickshaw driver to take me to the nearest restaurant. I was afraid that the driver wouldn't understand me properly, since I did not speak Hindi; the driver did not understand much English either. He drove for a half hour through the winding alleys of old Delhi, ended up in his own house, and asked his wife to prepare chapatti (Indian bread) and dhal (lentil curry). The house was small where he lived with his wife and child plus a cow. I was not the type who was afraid of human beings. Yet, there I was in Old Delhi at 11 pm in the house of a total stranger, with all the travel documents and one thousand two hundred dollars in my pocket. I was definitely a sitting duck. The lady of the house served the food very fast. The potato preparation and the dhal that accompanied the freshly made chapatti were heavenly. I wrote their address and kept it in my bag, and the driver took me back to the hotel around midnight. I thanked him for the extraordinary gesture of hospitality and paid him a decent sum of rupees for which he thanked me profusely. I slept deep like a tired farmer and woke up the next morning on time to reach for the orientation at NCERT.

We were a group of three, two girls and me. One was single but engaged to an American. The other was a Bengali and married. Her husband had come to bid her farewell. The orientation program consisted of talks on studies and life in the US. NCERT also checked if I was carrying the required number of dollars. The next day we flew to New York via Zurich and London. At the terminal in Zurich, I witnessed the strongest hailstorm that I had ever seen in my whole life. Hail stones of the size of tennis balls were falling on the glass windows of the airport with such force that I thought they would break. In London, the married girl and I stayed in the Cumberland Hotel near the Trafalgar Square. The other girl stayed with her uncle. I learnt to wear a tie through a self-instruction guide that I found in the hotel brochure. I had left New Delhi with a knot that betrayed my lack of skill in the matter. While strolling with the married girl in the Trafalgar Square after breakfast the next day, a photographer approached us and offered to take a picture as a souvenir of our visit to London. I thought it was a free, goodwill gesture from the English man, and allowed him to take the picture. My admiration to the Londoner doubled when he said that he would mail the picture to the US. Then he charged us three pounds. I had to pay, but the picture never reached us. I later realized that this was a common scam on tourists in many places around the world. There was probably not even film in the camera. We continued the journey in the afternoon and reached New York JFK airport around 2:00 pm. The date was 12th July, 1969. I had reached a world I had not even imagined in the wildest of my dreams. The airport looked big; so many planes arriving and departing, so many people coming and going, so many beautiful shops in the terminal, so many advertisements pleasing to the eyes, the long walk to the next terminal, the electro-mechanical stairs, etc, etc. I tried to contain my excitement so that I would not look like a village boy who had landed in the metropolis for the first time. We located the terminal and the gate from which the flight would take us to Minneapolis. I had crossed the Rubicon.

There was plenty of time in the terminal and in the plane to reminisce about my life: Where did I begin this journey? Where was I going? How did I fare so very differently from my nine siblings? Was it some special event in my life that had changed my course? As I look back, I had a very humble beginning, a nomadic life so to speak.

CHAPTER TWO

The Nomadic Beginning

My mother told me that I was born at sun-rise. In Kerala, India, that time can be any time between 6 and 7 am. I was born under a thatched roof into the hands of an old mid wife. No registration was made of my arrival, the way they do in the hospitals these days. On the seventh day, I was taken to the church to be baptized, and what the priest wrote in his registry is the only piece of information that saved me from anonymity. My parents named me Uduppan (a local Christian name for Joseph) in the church at baptism, but they called me Udup. The earliest recollection that I have is the accusing face of one of my uncles who caught me red handed for eating chunks of mud from the brick walls of my house. I was about two years old and yet the incident is vivid in my memory. My father beat me so that I never repeated that practice. However, I continued it whenever my father was out of sight. It was a sheer necessity, for my diet mostly consisted of rice, just carbohydrates. I suppose I was only compensating for the lack of some vital nutrients in my diet. Frankly, I don't have a scientific explanation for this behavior. Along the path of my life, I have met several people who ate mud in one form or another. The next thing I remember is the beatings I used to get from the teacher in the preparatory school, called Kalari, for not learning the alphabets in my native language, Malayalam, fast enough. The alphabets were written on sand, which I spread out on the class floor from a coconut shell, using my index finger. One can imagine how fast I learned the alphabets. I read the letters of the alphabet from a palm leaf written by the teacher and practiced them on the sand. The teacher wrote the letters on the leaf using a pointed metallic instrument and made them visible by applying a mixture of fine carbon powder and oil. As I write this story using the computer, I am amazed how far civilization has progressed in the last seventy years. I nick-named the teacher "fox," as he had the crafty face of a fox to manipulate and make the children learn and behave the way he wanted. I hated him, as he inspired fear in me. The fox teacher made sure that I completed the assignments by wielding and using the stick on me and reporting my performance to my father on a regular basis. What I liked most about the Kalari was the feast that the children gave on the day of their graduation. With the scarcity of food at home, anything served during graduation was relished, especially the sweets that we were all fond of. The graduation happened when one completed learning the alphabets and the numbers. Practically every month there was a graduation feast. My older brother graduated and went on to the first grade in the nearby primary school. The teacher of the Kalari said that I was almost ready for graduation, and, my father withdrew me to accompany my older brother to the school, so I did not graduate and had no feast. I was very sad for having lost the opportunity to celebrate my graduation and eat some good food. For many years, I would walk past the Kalari on my way to and from the primary school, and would resent and feel sad that my well-earned graduation was deprived of me for no fault of mine. I would look at the fox teacher as I passed by the Kalari and would get reminded of the pains I had gone through in his class.

At the time of my registration in the primary school, the principal asked for my birth date. My father gave an approximate date, which made me one year older than I really was. My father did this on purpose to make me legally eligible for admission to the first grade, although I looked small physically. Of course, the age of my older brother also had to be raised. Finally, both of us ended up sitting side by side on the same bench.

By this time, there were three boys in the family. Since the income from the land was meager, my mother worked in the neighboring houses. My father, too, worked for the neighbors to trim trees, cut down coconuts and jackfruits. Once, my father fell down from a jackfruit tree and broke both hands. He cried aloud from pain, and all the neighbors rushed to help him and carried him home. They thought it wise not to move him to the hospital far away, as he had to be carried on a stretcher for a good distance along footpaths. A local bone doctor appeared the next day and put straight sticks on the broken area, aligned the bones into place, and tied them with pieces cut from a towel. My father recuperated quickly, and resumed doing the same things he used to do. He was ambidextrous, something rare, as human beings tend to be defter using one hand or the other instead of both. He was very skilled at killing cobras. He used two sticks, one in each hand. While he raised the stick in the right hand for the cobra to look at, he struck it with the stick in the left hand. I was amazed by this trick played by my father. He used to impress me with his mathematical abilities too. He could recite the arithmetic table from memory, do the calculations in mind and resolve problems without paper and pencil. He was just a fourth grader, but he amazed me with his academic skills. Mother also was a fourth grader, and was good at reading. She used to read to us aloud passages from the Bible.

We moved into a house in a piece of land, bigger than the one on which we lived. My grandfather acquired this land for us, but we had to give back to him the land where we lived. I was four years old, and was excited to bathe every day in the river that bordered the land in the new place. The fourth boy was born in the new house. One day, a messenger came to inform my mother that my father was jailed for having stolen five rupees (not a small sum in those days) from a shop. My grandfather rushed to the jail, bailed him out, and gave him a good scolding. All the neighbors came to know of the incident, and my friends teased me for it. I felt ashamed that my father had been branded as a thief. When I walked on the street, some naughty neighbors called me names that alluded to my father being a thief. It pained me, and I stopped playing with my friends. The money was discovered in the shop itself, and no charge was filed against my father; in fact, the shopkeeper came to the house and apologized. I felt ashamed that I had misjudged my father. The neighbors stopped teasing me, and the whole incident was slowly forgotten. However, in the wake of this incident, heated discussions and exchange of accusations grew more frequent and louder between my father and mother. One day, I saw my father walk away, apparently to do an errand, but he did not come back in the evening. My mother grew alarmed, and asked for the protection of my grandfather, for she was afraid to stay alone with four children, the last one being just four months old and sick with measles. My grandfather stayed with us for all the two months that my father had gone away. Eventually, he appeared without giving an explanation to anyone, and resumed his duties. He had lost some respect in the family, and amongst the relatives and neighbors, for having run away leaving a wife with four small children. He performed his duties more earnestly, and compensated for his absence. He became more understanding with my mother and evaded unnecessary discussions with her, for a while.

One day, my parents noticed that my belly button was swollen, and took me to an herb doctor. He declared that my heart was small, the size of a chicken heart. My parents were alarmed and asked the doctor for urgent help. The doctor prescribed a cup of freshly extracted coconut toddy every morning before breakfast. I loved the taste of toddy and enjoyed the kick from it. Other herb concoctions were added to the treatment. Meat, fish, egg, and anything non-vegetarian were strictly forbidden. I had to be content with a bowl of rice while all the others in the family enjoyed a normal meal. I could not carry on for too long with the deprivation, and found the means of eating non-vegetarian items on the side. My belly button got more swollen, and I was rushed back to the doctor, who declared that I had broken the diet. My father gave me a good scolding in front of the doctor. The treatment continued, but with strict vigilance from my parents. Still, I found ways of eating the forbidden items without their knowledge. The sickness was not cured, and my parents gave up the treatment. They did not feel comfortable to take me back to the doctor, and I was left alone to eat whatever I wanted. I ate the normal diet, and the swelling eventually disappeared. My eating on the side had kept me alive, for I would have been totally famished had I not done that. However, my parents were concerned about the size of my heart, as told by the herb doctor. I heard comments from my parents that I was not destined to live long. As the river got flooded during the monsoon, we were practically isolated from our relatives for six months of the year. My mother could not live without the support and visits of her father, her two brothers and her sister, and eventually my family moved again, but to another plot of land adjoining the one we had left earlier. This plot was less hilly, and the walk to the school was less tiresome. I slowly got re-established and settled into my studies and helped my parents in minor chores.

My elder brother and I picked up fights often with other children from the school. We knew we could beat them up easily. On more than one occasion, the parents of the other children would come to our house to complain to my parents. My father questioned me and my elder brother in front of the accusing parents, and punished us there and then. Of course, my elder brother bore the brunt of the punishment. Our mother defended us in front of our father and the accusing parents. The next day, the children would tease us for having been punished, and we would pick up more fights. The fights in the school, along with my misbehaviors at home, led my father to warn me that he would tie me up on the beam, skin me, and put hot pepper all over my body. I took him seriously, and avoided all circumstances that would have led me to that fate. However, one day my father caught me red-handed for something, and tied my hands with a rope and lifted me up to the beam and asked my mother to bring a knife to flay me. She, of course, wouldn't bring the knife, and he shouted at her. She looked at him in disbelief, and I saw my father winking at her. I knew then that my father was not serious, that the whole thing was a hoax, and I remained calm. My father eventually brought me down, but warned me that next time it was going to be the real thing, and asked my mother to give me something to eat. On the whole, I should say that my father was a jolly good fellow. Of course, he had to keep several boys disciplined at home, and so resorted to all kinds of tricks. He never meant to harm us in any way whatsoever. He even played with us and bought us sweets when he returned from the market. He even used to kill some chickens and prepare good food for us when our mother was away visiting her father for a few days. When she returned, she noticed that a few chickens were missing, and my father would relate to her how the fox came at night and took away a few of them. Naturally, we encouraged our mother to visit her father more often.

In the summer months, I used to help my mother to carry water to the house from the river, almost a mile away. I was given a small vessel. Once, while I was climbing some steps with the vessel full of water, I lost balance, fell into the stream, and cut my chin. The neighbors rushed to my help by applying sugar and coffee powder to the wound. The blood stopped soon, but the coffee powder got stuck to the wound. It was dressed every day with more coffee powder, but I dreaded the process of removing the stuck powder, as it was painful. The wound healed soon, but left a scar that is visible even today. This scar has been used as identification mark in many documents, including my passport.

The fifth boy was born, and my mother sought help from her older sister for babysitting. My aunt sent her two girls in turn to look after us and the house, while my Mother was away for work in the neighboring houses. The elder one was Maria, and I used to call her affectionately Chechi, which in my language meant elder sister. Her younger sister was called Anna. We looked forward to their visits. The Chechis looked after us like a mother. Maria Chechi was reaching the age of marriage, and several proposals were considered and rejected. At last, one was accepted, and she was happily married at the age of eighteen. I was only six years old when she was married. I did not understand what was meant by marriage. I liked her getting married, because I liked a marriage feast, but I did not want her to go away after the marriage. I loved her for showing us unconditional love and dedication. Her food was delicious. Anna Chechi replaced Maria Chechi and looked after us with equal dedication. Six months after Maria Chechi's marriage, I could hear my mother and her mother whispering about her. I did not know what was happening. Eventually, I came to know that her husband had mistreated her. She was physically abused, and her mother used to cry in front of my mother for what was happening to her loving daughter. After living with her husband for five years, she returned home, physically exhausted, as she was suffering from tuberculosis. She was treated in her home by various physicians, quacks, and others.

My parents decided to move again to a place where more land was available for cultivation than what they had, in order to produce sufficient food for the growing family. In the new place, my mother could work in her own land and look after the children. My grandfather asked my father to go and look after the second share of land, which he had bought in a faraway place. The first share was being looked after by my uncle—my father's older brother. This uncle used to be back and forth from this far away place. He used to appear with his whole family and then disappear. Several of his children were older than me, and I used to like their company. So, when I was told that my cousins were to be my neighbors in the far-away land, I was elated. However, I was told that my elder brother and I were to stay behind to finish our school year. We were to stay with our grandparents. The prayers in the evening at our grandparent's house used to last an hour, and we had to be present to lead the session. It was hard to keep awake during the long recital. The good thing about it was that we were allowed to sit with our grandfather for dinner. We had the same food he ate, which was tasty and had extra dishes. After the dinner came the reading of the daily newspaper. One of us had to read the news to our grandfather, as he was illiterate. The Korean War was going on, and he wanted to know all about it. The reading session lasted at least an hour, and we used to fall asleep in front of him. Most of the time, he used to carry us to the bed. Our grandfather would wait with a stick for his youngest son, my uncle, to appear after spending the evening with his friends drinking. Occasionally, I would hear my uncle's cries of pains from the beating. His wife would serve him food and ease the pains. My grandfather never spared the rod on him if he came home drunk. Eventually, my uncle found the means of dodging him, by entering the house, secretly helped by his wife.

My parents moved, with the other three children, to the new place. Anna Chechi accompanied them. When they arrived, there was no one to inform them about the plot that was assigned to them. Whichever plot they put their feet into was claimed by another person in the group. My father did not know what to do, and was totally lost. He set up a thatched roof in a small bit of land which nobody had claimed, and started living there temporarily until things were sorted out. At this juncture, my mother casually met a person who was proposed to her for marriage years ago; the proposal fell through due to insufficient dowry. This person inquired about her situation, and when he found out that she had difficulty in finding a place to settle down, he offered to sell one of his pieces of land for a reasonable sum. The problem with the land was that it was hilly and not very accessible. Still, my parents accepted the deal, moved into the land, and erected a thatched hut. One week after they moved into the hut, a wild boar attacked them; Anna Chechi and my youngest brother were wounded. The boar pierced the thigh of Anna Chechi and the neck of my brother, who was just four years old. It is a miracle that both of them survived. My father came back to look for both of us. I saw a train for the first time, and was amazed at the sheer size of it and the fire that I saw in the steam engine. We got down at a station at five in the morning and walked with our entire luggage on our heads through the track to a boat jetty nearby. We took a boat and reached close to five miles from our house, where we started walking. At some point, my father had to carry me and my piece of luggage too, as I got tired of walking. We reached home late in the evening after climbing the steep hill. I felt that heaven was closer. I was told about the wild boar attack, and I saw the scars of the wound on my brother's neck. Anna Chechi had returned to her house before we reached.

It was a place where there were wild monkeys, hyenas, wild tortoises, and fowls in the nearby forests. I remember, one day, the people of the village, caught a tiger, which used to attack the domestic animals in a cage. It was ferocious and jumped at the people who went to see it. I also remember that I had to carry my lunch to school and eat it secretly if it contained meat, as many children in the school were orthodox Hindus, who were vegetarians and did not appreciate people eating meat. My family members were meat eaters from birth, but I was careful not to offend the sentiments of the Hindus who lived around us in this new place. One incident that I remember clearly is as follows. Before I moved to the new place, I had a friend who suddenly became very pious. He used to attend mass every day and became an altar boy. Everybody used to comment that he was preparing to join the seminary. Some people even said that Our Lady of Fatima had appeared to him. The statue of Our Lady of Fatima had just passed through our village. Some people who visited his house found him kneeling and praying in front of a statue of the Blessed Virgin in a corner of the house. I, too, wanted to see the Blessed Virgin. I prayed that the Blessed Virgin would appear to me on a tree near a stream down my new house. I would kneel in front of the tree, close my eyes, and pray for the appearance of the Blessed Mother. Nothing happened, except that I saw a few monkeys looking at me strangely from the tree. I reaffirmed my faith and re-doubled my prayers, to no avail. Eventually, I gave up the futile practice. My friend continued his practice of piety for a few more years. He used to collect the money that people deposited at the feet of the Blessed Virgin. When he had accumulated a certain amount, he gave up going to church, and set up an illegal liquor business. He was caught and put in the jail, where he stayed a few years. The devil has many forms to deceive people.

After one year, my parents suddenly decided to return to our former place. It happened this way: my parents had planted yucca and when it was ready to harvest, gave it on contract to a local businessman. This person came with his workers and pulled out the plants. In the process, a good part of the produce stayed in the ground. The businessman complained that the yield was not what he had expected, and that he wouldn't pay the sum that was agreed upon. My parents decided to stop the logs that were pulled through our land, which belonged to him, until the sum was paid. Some neighbors promised that they would help us to stop the logs. However, my mother was afraid that the businessman would resort to violence, and would hurt my father. She asked my father to return to our former land and wait for the whole problem to be resolved. I was asked to accompany my father. Thus, both of us left, and my mother and four brothers stayed back. The businessman got news of the plot, and resolved the problem peacefully. He paid the full amount to my mother and took away whatever he obtained from the yucca plantation. My father returned to look for my mother and my brothers. Volumes can be told from this incident about the personalities of my father and mother. While my mother squarely faced problems, my father found ways to avoid them. I cannot pat my back either, since I had left the scene. I have the excuse that I was only eleven years old; still, I honestly have to admit that I too behaved like a coward.

I lost one year, as I left the last school without completing the year. The move was even more disastrous for my elder brother. He stopped going to school in order to look after the younger ones while my parents went to work. I ended up in the same grade I had been studying when I left. I felt humiliated, as I had to study with children who were in the lower grade when I left. The boys with whom I used to fight had graduated from the school, and had gone to another. I did not pick any more fights, as I didn't have the support from my elder brother. I became a serious student. My father was strict with the grades. In those days, the pass mark was 35 percent, but my father used to beat me for every subject for which I got less than 50 percent. I made sure that my grades were good so that I wouldn't get beaten. My mother was not allowed to sign my report card. My family settled down in a place my parents bought by the side of a road. The walk to the school was shorter. The house needed renovation. We tore it down and built a modest new house in its place. We could not afford anything better. The buses would stop right in front of the house for us to go anywhere. There was a river behind the house, which had plenty of water and fish throughout the year. I enjoyed fishing, and brought fish to the house for my mother to make a curry dish out of it. When it rained heavily, the water level almost would reach the back porch of our house, and I could fish from there.

I resumed going to the house of my grandparents to sleep over, lead the prayers, and read the newspaper. Grandma suffered from asthma, and she used to take opium to get some relief from this sickness. Whenever she opened the bottle of opium she used to give me some to taste. I never liked the bitter taste of opium, and never got high on it, as I consumed very little quantity. But, eventually I liked it, and tasted it often for almost three years. I graduated from the fifth grade and went to a private school run by the sisters of our parish, where I could study the sixth, seventh and eighth grades. The sisters were strict disciplinarians, and taught us catechism every Sunday. I could not escape catechism on Sundays, as the sisters were very watchful. Eventually, I learned to escape the class by simply going to another church. The sisters would question me as to why I didn't turn up to our church for mass, and I would invent all kinds of excuses for going to another church.

My mother had a delivery almost every two years, and all were boys. She wanted a girl desperately, for she was of the opinion that girls understood and supported the mother more than boys did. Probably that is true, but she was unlucky and eventually ended up with ten boys. As I was second in the line, I was asked to help out in the house with chores, and even in the field. The work load increased as the years went by. I used to lift heavy loads, beyond my physical capacity. I used to muster all my adrenaline and carry the load. As a result, my vertebral column bent to one side, as I found it out in my adult age. The work at home reached to a point when I could not find time to do the home-work; my home-work time was one hour before the school, seated on a rubber tree, in a secluded area. There, I would memorize a poem in one reading; I would complete all the home-work assignments in one sitting. I would even find time to smoke a beedi (a popular and cheap substitute for cigarette very much used in India even today) before the classes began, and reminisce about life and its problems and its mysteries. In one of these sessions, suddenly out of the blue sky, it occurred to me how human reproduction happened. Nobody had told me about it. I still wonder how I could imagine on my own all that happened in the bed between a man and a woman. I think nature just reveals it. I have no other answer. Somewhere at this time, I became aware that I liked a girl who was the daughter of our neighbor. She studied in my class, and we walked together to the school. Her mother and my mother were good friends. Her name was Leela. She was fair and good looking. I enjoyed her company, and she felt the same way in my company. Her mother sometimes joked to my mother that we would make a good pair in the future. There were social taboos, which limited us, from manifesting our liking toward each other, and our parents kept close watch on us so that we didn't cross the red line.

I acquired the habit of smoking beedi very early in life, as a child. My father prohibited me from smoking it, but I made sure that my father never caught me doing that. He had his suspicions, and was on the lookout, but I was always cautious. My father even asked the sisters in the school to be on the lookout if I smoked. He came to school every Wednesday on his way to the local market and checked with the sisters on my performance in studies and my behavior at school. The sisters did not have much to tell my father. They used to come near me to smell my breath, but I always chewed a leaf after a smoke that masked the breath for hours. One day, I came a little early to the school, as I had a lot of homework to do. I went to the usual secluded place behind the school, where nobody would find and disturb me. While doing the homework, I smoked a beedi. Suddenly, a sister appeared right in front of me. As I did not want the sister to catch me right in the act of smoking, I threw the but away at one stroke. But what could I do with the smoke that was already in my mouth? I swallowed it and got choked. The sister came running to help me get the smoke out of my lungs by tapping my back. I was coughing a lot while trying to exhale the smoke quickly through my mouth and nose. The timely intervention of the sister alleviated my pain. She shared the incident with the headmistress sister, who asked me to go into her office. There, she gave me a few canings but never told my father about the incident. The sisters wanted to gain my goodwill, as I was considered a leader whom they could count on for any job at school. I was a good student and was involved in every extracurricular activity at school. The sisters counted on me to act in a drama, recite a poem, make a speech, lead the children to carry stones for the construction of our parish church, and even decorate the school for a function. They did not consider it prudent to report all of my bad behaviors to my father, risking my alienation from such activities. In fact, they gave mostly good reports of me. I stood first in most of the subjects in the exams. The subject that I disliked most was Mathematics, mostly because it was taught by a nun who did not understand it either. She taught the children how to resolve problems, but did not explain the underlying logic of the subject. I did well in the exams in Math because I learnt the tricks to resolve the problems, but never understood their rationale. I was always afraid that the day would come when I would have to demonstrate in-depth knowledge of the subject. Although I was first in all subjects, a classmate of mine decided that he would compete with me for grades; in fact, he beat me in several subjects, but I retained the number one position. Eventually, the boy gave up competing with me, as his father was a drunkard and never supported or appreciated his grades. On the other hand, my father always appreciated my performance at school, and even repeated some of the good feedback he received from the sisters in front of the whole family, including my grandparents.

On the way back from school, I used to jump into a river and play with some friends. My father had prohibited me from getting into the river, especially during the monsoon season, because he was afraid

I would drown. He also wanted me to return to the house without wasting time, as there was enough work waiting for me. Still, I jumped quite often. Once, I did not quite make it to the other side, and started drinking water. My friends were nearby, and thought I was playing by going down and coming up, and so did not bother. Fortunately, the current took me to shallow water, but the few seconds were enough for me to confess to God all the sins I had committed, especially the many lies I had told my parents. They never came to know about the incident, lest they prohibit me completely from getting into the river, and so I continued the practice as long as I was in school.

Anna Chechi came to the house regularly to look after the children, and was like a second mother. Soon, she too got married and went away. We felt orphaned, but I liked her husband. They often came to the house, and my father used to kill a pig for the occasion. He was very skilled at that. He used to hold the pig between his toes and strike the pig on the head. It was not a good sight to watch, but who questions age old customs, especially when you are child?

I was about to graduate from seventh grade, and after one more year, I was to go to high school. My parents wondered how they could afford to pay for my high school and the education of my younger brothers, and feed so many mouths at the same time. In one of her visits to her father's house, my mother visited her uncle, Kurian, and discussed with him her predicament regarding my education. He promised that he would look for a viable solution. Not very long after, he came to our house and informed us that I could be sent to a boarding school in the neighboring state, run by a religious congregation of Brothers. I did not know anything about religious congregations or Brothers, and neither my parents nor Uncle Kurian; we only knew about priests. Uncle Kurian informed us that the boarding school was run for the purpose of promoting vocations for the Brotherhood. I told my parents that I did not want to become a Brother. I did not want to go away leaving behind my parents and brothers. I was just fourteen, and wanted to be with my family and enjoy my friends' company. My father assuaged my fears and assured me that I would not be sent away against my wishes. However, he insisted that I go through with the selection interview. I accepted, thinking that I would not be selected. Accordingly, I was interviewed by a Brother in a town quite far from my house. The Brother looked at my marks and seemed impressed from his looks. He selected me immediately, although he never selected boys who hadn't completed the eighth grade, and I was only going into the eighth grade. I was an obvious exception. The Brother explained about the school, the boarding life and facilities, and the journey by a special train to the Nilgiris Hills town known as Coonoor, where the School was located. He also carefully explained the purpose of the free schooling and boarding. He was careful to explain in detail the many facilities the school had for playing games, which impressed me. I did not raise much objection to going to the boarding school, as the thought of playing games caught my attention. My mother was visibly happy that I was selected and that I was willing to try the experience. Uncle Kurian was present during the interview, and explained to me all the good things about the program. The medium of education was Tamil, the language of the neighboring state, and I had to learn it. This made me feel a little jittery, yet I decided to stick with the decision to go. It was already June; the schools had already re-opened and I had to rush through the goodbyes to my dear ones. I went to the house of Leela to bid farewell to her. She did not understand why I was going away. I tried to explain to her that I was going to study in a boarding school, but she did not get the reason behind it. I did not explain that the purpose of the boarding school was religious vocation. She was sad that I was leaving her. I assured her that I would come back and see her. Maria Chechi insisted that she would come to bid me farewell the morning I was to take the bus that would take me to the train station. We woke up early, as the bus was to come at 8 am. The local head of the Communist Party, who was a friend of the family, came early in the morning and advised my father not to send me away. He explained that I would be treated like one among many sheep in the heard. That made my mother a little nervous about sending me away, but still she stuck to the plan. The iron suitcase was already packed, my relatives had come to bid me farewell, and the bus was to come soon. There was no backing down. I saw Maria Chechi running as the bus passed her. She had barely turned the corner when the bus came and stopped. She continued running to see me, but the bus didn't stop for her. Through the back window, I saw her falling down as she doubled her speed. Later, I came to know that she was taken to the hospital for bruises. Not long after, she died peacefully, and I could see her only in her funeral photos. Even to-day, after more than fifty years, her running to the bus and falling down still lingers in my mind. Anna Chechi, too, cried before and after I left. I, too, let out a few tears, but was careful not to show all my emotions in front of the other passengers. My mother was stoic, as she did not want to betray her real feelings lest I resist going away. She broke down as I left, and for a long time it was repeated after reading my letters. My father accompanied me to the train station to hand me over to the Brother. The train came and parting from my father was very sad. I cried, but stopped abruptly as I noticed three other boys in the train looking at me with empathy. They had boarded a few stations before, and were going to the same place. We all wondered what was happening to us. Why were we separated from our parents, brothers, sisters and relatives?

CHAPTER THREE

The Nilgiris Express

The Brother was an expert in dealing with separation. He bought us food that we liked to eat. We had to change three trains to reach our destination. The last train was The Nilgiris Express. It climbed through the hills at no more than twenty miles per hour. It crossed several tunnels and tea estates. The scenery of the tea estates was picturesque, as they appeared like a spread-out green carpet. The tunnels were scary as they were totally dark. We reached the station and were met by other Brothers from the boarding school. The drive to the boarding school lasted fifteen minutes. The boarding had about hundred and fifty kids. They welcomed us with curiosity, compassion and even with a little bit of ragging. I felt that I had ended up in a strange world that I had never imagined. There were children from all parts of South India speaking different languages; they all came in separate batches and for the same purpose. The Brothers were of Indian and European origin. The garden all around us looked luscious and contained many flowers I had never before seen. I became an instant curiosity, as I was the only one in the boarding to study in the eighth grade. We were shown around and each assigned a desk in the study room and a bed in the dormitory. Soon we were running around with other kids, and the trauma of separation from parents and relatives slowly ebbed away. The Director of the Boarding was a Canadian Brother who was very pleasant with whom to talk. I did not understand him for he spoke English, but his face was friendly. The food in the dining room was strange and very different from what I was used to at home. I wrote to my parents of my arrival, the food and the boarding life. My mother took notice of only the food part and concluded that I was given food not fit for human consumption; she could not think of any food different from what she served at home. Nevertheless, my father wrote back to tell me to try it out for some time, and if I did not like my stay, I could return home. After a while, I learnt to like the food which was more abundant and nutritious, but less tasty than what I ate at home. I wrote back to my parents that I would stay as there were many plusses to the boarding life.

The boarders got up early in the morning, had prayers and walked twenty minutes to the local church for Mass. Occasionally; there was Mass in our chapel if a priest was available. In December, the ground froze to zero degrees, and I found the walk difficult as I walked barefooted. I got frost bitten very soon. I wrote to my parents and asked them to send me some money to buy a pair of slippers. Even with my wearing slippers, the icy road made my feet cold. After Mass, there was some time for studies, followed by breakfast and gardening.

After a quick shower and some more study time, the classes began in the school. The school was attended by approximately four hundred boys from the locality along with hundred and fifty from the boarding. After school, there was one hour for games which helped me get over my home sickness. I loved to play football and became quite good at it.

The school was well known in the hill town, although there was another school better known for its English medium and European teachers; this school was run by another congregation of Brothers. The boys who studied there were regular boarders from rich families. They were well dressed and had snobbish looks. I would see them occasionally in inter school sports or in the church on Sundays; we sometimes crossed each other on week-end walks. There was also a boarding school for girls run by Sisters. The girls from this school could be seen only in the church. I couldn't concentrate much during the Mass as I looked their way very often.

I found it difficult in the beginning to follow the classes in a language different from my mother—tongue, but I caught up with it in three months time. Soon I began to compete with a studious boy from the locality for the first rank. I particularly liked drawing and painting and got good grades in them, while my competitor outperformed me in mathematics and language. In internal exams, drawing and painting counted, and the competition between me and my academic rival was neck to neck. Another subject to which I paid scant attention was Hindi, the national language, which was optional. One could fail in the subject and yet pass the year-end exams and get promoted to the next grade. The Hindi teacher was the most miserable teacher in school because very few children paid any attention to the subject as it was not compulsory. Then, why was it taught in the school in the first place? As the national language, it had to be taught by law in all the schools. Later in my adult life, I would feel sorry that I neglected it as I loved to hear the language spoken because it sounded very pleasing to the ears. Many of my friends would speak it, and I would feel sorry that I couldn't understand it.

Six months after I arrived, I started growing hair in the places where a man usually has them. I was not aware of what was happening to me. There was no one I could turn to for advice. I felt erections and loved to see a girl. However, there were no girls around, except the convent girls who were practically cloistered; I enjoyed looking at them the few times they were in the church. I was selected to act as young Jesus in the scene where He got lost in the temple, and His parents were looking for him. The girl from the convent who acted as the Blessed Virgin was very beautiful; I loved to play my part and looked forward for the practice sessions, which was always held in the convent. I felt bad when the play was over, and the opportunity to visit the convent was gone. The next year, I was called to act as the devil that tempted Jesus in the desert after the forty days of fasting. That play was practiced in my School, but staged in the convent. I still wonder what to make of me acting one year like Jesus and the next year like the devil. Did I have both personalities—God and the Devil—inherited by birth or developed by social interaction? I did not know what I had projected all these years, the Jesus or the devil in me.

I broke my left hand while playing volley-ball. I was taken to the local hospital by the Brothers, and the hand was plastered. The physiotherapy to straighten out the hand was very painful. The fact that I had to sit out the games during one month was still more painful. I made up for it after I returned to the courts. We played football barefoot. Once, a boy kicked my legs accidentally. The bruise became blue after a few days. Very soon it became like gangrene. I was hospitalized and had surgery performed on me. I was aware of drops of chloroform solution that were placed on the face mask that made me unconscious. When I woke up, the doctor explained that a lot of puss was drawn out from the wound. In the hospital, I met a young man who was suffering from bone cancer. I did not understand what was meant by cancer. The young man had had several previous operations to remove several ribs. He had gradually lost the effect of anesthesia, and the operations were very painful. I felt very bad that he suffered a lot; however, he learnt to endure everything and projected a happy face. I accompanied him for walks, which were painful for him, within the hospital premises. I felt badly leaving him behind when I left the hospital. However, I still wonder why nobody visited him while I was there. Soon, I was back in the hospital, this time in the isolation ward for chickenpox. There were five other boys from the boarding who accompanied me. We played chess and caroms to while away time. The nurses brought us some of the leftover food that we devoured. We were happy that we didn't have to attend school. When we left after two weeks, we wished we had had a second attack. My parents could not understand why I had been hospitalized so many times. Two consecutive letters to them were written from the hospital. My mother even asked my father to bring me back home as she thought I was sick and weak. My father kept his cool.

After one and a half years, I was allowed to go home for a short visit during Christmas vacations. My father came to look for me at the train station. I was very excited to see my parents and brothers. My mother wept tears of joy. Some of the younger brothers seemed not to recognize me; they had been smaller when I had left. There was even a new arrival, another boy, the ninth in the line. I had grown taller and had begun growing hairs on my face. My mother had prepared all types of food and wanted me to eat as much as I could. She wanted to compensate for all the food that she couldn't serve me for the last one and a half years. Leela came to see me, and her happiness was visible on her face. She discreetly entreated me not to go back. My paternal grandmother and paternal grandfather had passed away during my absence. I proudly showed some cups that I had won in the boarding school for outdoor games. My mother really did not understand what they were for because I found her using some of them for serving food. Besides, there wasn't a show case at home to display them. Although I had learnt to like the boarding school, I declared to my mother one week after I had arrived that the food was bad and that I was not going back. The underlying reason was that I didn't want to become a religious Brother. She told me that I didn't have any future at home and that there was one more mouth to feed. She thought I was doing well in the boarding school and recommended that I should return, especially since she could not afford to pay for my education at the high school level. I insisted that I did not want to go back, that I would help the parents in whatever way I could to make both ends meet. My father had no opinion. He had learnt the hard way not to contradict his wife. After many discussions, finally, I got convinced that my future was away from home, and, so I went back to the boarding school after a month of vacations. My mother packed me some homemade sweets which I shared with my friends who couldn't go home. After a few days of being home-sick, I settled into my studies once again.

I was selected to play football for my school, but I could not play well with kids from the neighboring school: they were playing with shoes while I was playing barefooted. I was frightened when some big boys from the government school, with shoe nails projecting out, charged at me. Later it was found that these players were not really students, but unemployed young men. However, I was a player to be reckoned with amongst the boarding school boys. Still, a sense of insecurity, a feeling that I was going to be smaller in stature than my peers brought me some melancholic moments. I could not blame my parents for my height as they too were short by inheritance. I decided to play tough to make up for the shortness. I decided not to reveal my inner insecurity to the outside world, to appear bigger than what I really was, to be a poker face, to be a chameleon. It is an instinct in many animals, as a way of self defense, to show themselves, in one of many ways, to be more than what they really are. They may puff up physically, mimic the cry of a more ferocious animal and change their color to a more aggressive tone or adapt the posture of a bigger animal. I decided to make up by impressing people through my speech and gestures. Accordingly, as a first strategy, I decided to have a better command of the English language as I found out that those who were good at it were very much admired. I started learning the meaning of at least ten words per day. There were days when I even memorized one page from the dictionary. Very soon I felt more comfortable in the use of the English, especially speaking it. The spoken language of the boarding school was mostly English as the boys had to interact frequently with the European Brothers who supervised them. Soon I became comfortable speaking with these Brothers. I looked around for English novels, but could find only a limited number of them. Hence, I read whatever material that came my way. I scored almost hundred percent in the English exams.

During the long summer holidays, the Director of the boarding school organized games to keep the boys occupied. The games were held in three areas: outdoor sports, indoor games (chess, caroms, etc.), and intellectual games. I was the aggregate winner of any one or two of the above categories for three years, and in the final year, I won all three of them. This fact, coupled with being first in the class, raised my self-esteem greatly. I began to feel confident to handle any problem that I would face in life. Self esteem is the most valuable gift that one can inherit or develop in life. I even became overconfident, and this was one of my major defects. Too much of a good thing is bad.

I went home for a second time during the last year of my studies during Christmas vacations. As soon as I reached home, my parents told me that they had sold the little property we lived on and exchanged another property we had for ten acres of forest land in Malabar, the northern most part of Kerala, infested with malaria and other diseases. They told me that they had to do it for more land for cultivation. The move was planned in a month, as soon as I returned after vacations. I understood their decision to look for more land to cultivate and feed the eight boys who were growing bigger. I did not welcome the idea of getting uprooted, getting cut off from my friends and relatives. Leela was engaged for marriage to a boy three years older to me. I felt the loss of her, but conformed to my fate. I felt she too was disappointed that our relationship had come to nothing and that she was getting married to somebody she didn't know. I raised with my parents the idea of not going back to school and accompanying them to Malabar. My mother advised me to continue with my studies; she told me that I may be the only one to study in the family as other children might drop out in the process of conquering the Malabar jungles. I saw my mother's argument as reasonable and decided to return. I had intended to tell them that I didn't want to become a religious Brother and that I planned to be on my own after graduation; However, I didn't tell them so, knowing that it would upset them even more as they were already anxious as to how they were going to fare in an unknown place. I would have given them unnecessary worry if I had gone with them or revealed my intentions. I left with a heavy heart, knowing that my parents were suffering and that I was leaving behind my birthplace with so many roots, so many friends, and so many memories. I sobbed quietly in the train and vowed someday I would return to my parents and alleviate their sufferings. The next three months were crucial as I had to write the finals. The grades I got in the exams opened or closed the doors of my future and would make or break my life. Everywhere in India, one carried along the High School Certificate that contained all the marks one had obtained in one's school life. Fortunately, I had good marks in all subjects except Hindi as mentioned earlier. Additionally, my English grades stood out for everyone to see and admire.

One day, the Brothers informed the boys that the Russians had sent the Sputnik into space to orbit around the earth and that they had scored a decisive victory over the Americans in conquering outer space. I did not understand anything about the technical aspect of the event. I wondered how the Sputnik could go around the earth without falling down. I asked around and did not get a satisfactory answer from anyone. The final exams arrived, and I was well prepared for them. I wrote all the exams well with the exception of Hindi. It was a subject that I had to write, but not necessarily pass. I did not know much about the subject as I had neglected it. I just copied the questions into the answer paper with the intent to fill up pages. I then wrote the numbers from one to ten in Hindi, which was not even asked as an answer. When the results came, I had good marks in all the subjects except Hindi, in which I scored ten marks out of hundred. I couldn't understand how I even got ten marks; I should have obtained a zero. May-be the examiner had given me some grace marks in Hindi just not to make me feel too bad. The Hindi marks, however, brought my average down, and I did not get the first rank in the school which the Brothers expected from me. I felt like a fool that had dropped the ball. It was to me a lesson in life.

After the exams, I informed the Brothers that I was not going to join them. They did not look too disappointed either; all along the way, I hadn't shown much inclination to be a Brother. I hadn't shown any aversion to that possibility either; as I was afraid they would send me away. The Director of the boarding school let me leave peacefully, without exacting payment for any expense incurred during the four years of my stay there. Nevertheless, where would I go? If I returned to my parents, I would end up in limbo without the possibility to continue my studies. I had become unused to working on the land. I wanted to go and help them settle down, but I was afraid I only would add to their worries. I took the return Nilgiris Express not knowing where to end my journey. In a way, the Nilgiris Express was a witness to my joys, sadness, doubts, misgivings, uncertainties, hope and courage. As the train stopped at the last station, I continued the journey in yet another train, not knowing where I was heading. This train ended up in a big station through which several important trains passed. I enquired about the next train to arrive, which was the Madras Mail. I decided to take it and end my journey at Madras (now called Chennai), the capital of the state of Tamil Nadu. I was a ticketless traveler as I did not have enough money to buy one. I was anxious as I did not wish to be caught by the Ticket Collector (TC). Fortunately, I could evade the TC amongst so many other travelers, but I could not afford to sleep. I did not know anybody in Madras. I did not know what I would do as I had no plans. I did not have any money.

Nevertheless, I felt like a bird freed from a cage, free to go anywhere and do as I pleased. Freedom is the most precious gift of a human being. I did not know what I was to do with my freedom as I was used to limits being all around me. I was exposed to many perils in the street due to my lack of experience in the real world; but my poker face stood me in good stead. I felt confident that no challenge was beyond my capacity. I was prepared to face them.

CHAPTER FOUR

Learning the Hard Way

I got into a restaurant near the railway station not knowing where to go. I overheard the owner talking to his friend; he was looking for someone to tutor his two sons. The tutor was to teach the boys sixth grade English and Math. I approached him and offered to tutor his boys, and after much questioning, my offer was accepted. The owner let me live in his outhouse for a few days. He also provided me with food until I moved into my own place. After a week of tuition, he paid me some money. I had put all my interest into teaching his children. I thought he saw it that way, too for him to reward me. The money was put to good use to rent a room. I continued to teach the boys, and I was paid generously, yet not enough to eke out a living, let alone continue my studies at the University. I wrote a long letter to Uncle Kurian explaining the reasons for my not joining the Brotherhood and requesting a loan to continue my studies. Uncle Kurian was a strange person. He lived with his sister and nephew. His sister had lost her husband, and Uncle Kurian had separated from his wife several years earlier. His past was never discussed at home as it was a delicate subject. He and his sister decided to live under the same roof and support each other. I knew that Uncle Kurian had the means to support me, but was unsure whether he would respond positively. To my surprise, Uncle Kurian replied saying that he empathized with me and that he would support me in whatever way he could. He said that he would not be able to pay for all the costs of my education, but he would contribute significantly to it. He had not specified any amount. I was elated with the reply and applied to several colleges for admission. I was admitted at Loyola College for a one year pre-university course. I wrote to Uncle Kurian informing him about the admission, and he, in turn, sent enough money to pay for the first tuition installment. I still had to find the means to pay for my boarding and lodging. I continued tutoring the children, and more children belonging to the relatives of the family began using my service. I extended tuition to the friends of the children, and finally I was in a position to pay for my lodging and boarding. By this time, I had my own shanty to hold private tuition classes. I had to be careful with my expenditures as I could not afford any extravagances. I started attending college in all earnest and studied very hard.

I wrote to my parents explaining the reason why I had moved to Madras. I also comforted them by explaining how I had become independent economically. They thanked Uncle Kurian for his support and requested him to supervise my studies. Uncle Kurian made a personal visit to check on me. He also visited the college where I was studying and duly informed my parents about my life. My parents were comforted by his letter and began to worry less about me. Uncle Kurian left after one week and gave me some money to pay for the second tuition installment.

I found mathematics very difficult as I had not taken the advanced course in high school. I must have been the only student in the class who hadn't taken the course. The teacher had presumed that all the students in his class were at the same base level. I was far behind the rest of the class, and as the teacher proceeded with his lessons, I found myself totally lost. The foreboding feeling that math would come back to haunt me became a reality. Since I planned to major in a science subject at the degree level, mathematics was obligatory, and I had to perform well in the subject in order to get admitted for the degree course. With alarm bells ringing in my head, I knew I had to find a quick solution. I decided to concentrate on mathematics. Fortunately, I could afford to pay less attention to English. The second language was French, which was easy, too. Hence, I gave all my attention to mathematics. I could not afford to pay for a tutor and, decided to learn on my own. I decided to start from the basics. I bought some high school self-study guides and worked out the problems. The advanced level was tough, but I kept at it until I felt comfortable with it. The more problems I worked out, the easier the subject became and the more motivated I felt. In two months, I reached the same level as the rest of the class. My efforts had paid off, and my self-esteem rose once again.

I got letters from my older brother informing me that my parents had difficulties settling down in the new place. They had not seen the land before they bought it, and when they saw it, they were disappointed. It was hilly and rocky and required a lot of labor. It had also been given as two separate plots. My parents cultivated one of the two plots for a whole year before they exchanged both for a single plot of ten acres. In the process, they gave away for free all the cultivation they had done for one year. They began to work earnestly on the new plot and cultivated several items for daily food as well as for long-term sustenance. They even sent me a basket of ripe bananas, which were delicious. I grew anxious to visit them after my exams before I started my degree program. Soon, the tenth boy was born in the family, and I was anxious to see him. The exams were easy, and I went home for the summer break. My parents had become very thin from all the hard work. Some of my younger brothers were attending local schools and were playful students. The question came up as to what they would do after high school. Nobody had a clue. Two of my younger brothers had quit studies, and I saw them carry basket loads of banana to the market to support the family. These loads were obviously much beyond their capacity. I had pity for them, but the money was necessary for the house-hold expenses. Originally being a forest, our land was the feeding ground for wild elephants. In fact, elephants still came up to the border of our land. We were afraid that the elephants would cross over and attack us. In fact, one elephant came at mid-night to the house of a friend, knocked down the roof, stomped its way into the house and crushed to death the head of the family without harming his wife or the child who were sleeping next to him. This person had shot and hurt the same elephant two months before in an attempt to get its tusks. The animal was on the lookout for vengeance and did so without raising the least suspicion from even the closest neighbors. This incident proves that elephants indeed have a great memory. Even today, some of my brothers continue to live in the same land and often hear the cry of the elephants in the reserve forest, beyond the river. I stayed the full summer with my family and returned to Madras for my degree studies. I had obtained a first class in the exams and gained admission for undergraduate studies in the same college to major in Chemistry. The fees were higher for the degree studies, and Uncle Kurian yet again offered to increase his contribution. I added more children for tuition and earned more money.

I would have loved to be an engineer or a doctor, but as I was unable to afford to study these professions, I didn't even consider them. The Head of the Chemistry Department was a post-graduate from Princeton University and a well-known Researcher. He taught Organic Chemistry to our class, but the boys couldn't understand him. He was an eminence in his subject, but a poor teacher. The class protested, and we were assigned to another lecturer who was a Ph.D. This professor turned out to be worse than the previous one. He too was a specialist in the subject, but couldn't teach it well. He would write a complicated problem on the board and ask the class to solve it. When none of us could solve it, he would solve it himself and make us feel stupid. The students complained, and we were quickly assigned another professor called Prakasam who had just completed his Master's degree in the same college. He was an excellent lecturer, and we loved his teaching and his attitude to help. I learned a lot of chemistry from him, and soon he became my role model. One of the students in my class wanted to make his own fire cracker for Deepavali, a well-known festival in Madras during which a lot of fire crackers are exploded. During the lab experiments, this student stole some sodium peroxide and tucked it away into his pant pocket. When the sodium peroxide absorbed moisture, it exploded, and his pants caught fire. The boy was standing by my side, and it became my duty to put off the fire. The flame burnt bright yellow because of its sodium content. I tore down his pant leg to save his life. The student was rushed to the hospital and eventually discharged. He never returned. This incident impacted me a great deal.

I continued to go home every summer to help my parents with the cultivation. I loved the lush green forest as far as the eye could see. I would go fishing in the river bordering the forest. I caught plenty of fresh fish and shared the catch with all the neighbors. My mother used to fall sick very often, owing to the cold climate and the mental stress to feed so many children. She worked very hard and managed everything at home. My father had faith in my mother's intuitions and let her manage matters both in and outside the home. He worked very hard every day and never worried for the morrow. My mother took care of both, today and tomorrow. One day my mother handed over twenty rupees to my father to buy rations. As he got into the street, one of the neighbors came running, requesting some money to take his child with a high fever to the doctor. My father gave him the twenty rupees. He went to the ration shop and purchased the rice on credit. After two months, the neighbor returned the money to my mother, and asked to thank my father for having loaned him the money to save his son. It was only then that we came to know my father had helped the neighbor and purchased the ration grains on credit. All the neighbors were recipients of his generosity, advice and even his money; they deeply respected him. However, he was not a prophet in his own house. Scarcity is never a companion of generosity. As soon as I left home, my father too left. Nobody knew where he had gone. Soon the tea shop owner from the neighboring village showed up at our door to take away the cow we owned. My father had eaten at his shop on credit. He had sold the cow away secretly to pay the credit and left the village with the difference. My mother refused to hand over the cow as she heavily depended on it for the milk for her children. However, the neighbors intervened and convinced her to hand over the animal. For two months, my father never appeared. He had left the family with other debts, too, and my mother had to repay them one by one. We quietly hoped that he would privately inquire if the debts were paid off and would slip into the house as quietly as he had disappeared as if nothing had ever happened. However, this time he went away for more than two months, and we got worried. My mother asked my older brother to search for him in and around the Malabar area. The area being very vast, searching for him was like looking for a needle in a hay stack. My brother was reluctant to undertake this mission. At the insistence of our mother, he offered to look for him. He thought of concentrating his search in and around areas previously frequented by our father. For one week, he went around asking acquaintances and strangers but to no avail. Finally, he went to another area where he knew nobody. He asked around giving physical descriptions of our father and was told that such a person had been seen in that area just the day before. He was told to enquire with the nearby estate owner as he regularly employed contracted workers. It was evening, and my brother was walking to the estate; Lo and behold, our father was coming the opposite way, walking towards the river to bathe after the day's work. He readily accompanied my brother, and when they reached home, he quietly occupied himself in the regular chores as though nothing had happened. Initially he did not speak with anyone unless spoken to, but soon, settled down into his daily routine. Soon, he became the old jovial person who made everybody laugh. The villagers were very happy that he had returned as he was their counselor during problems and an angel during economic need, even at the cost of sacrifices for his own family.

I enjoyed my studies thoroughly at Loyola College. I had excellent professors for most subjects. There was nobody better than Fr. Seguera to teach English Literature. His Shakespeare classes were utterly enjoyable. Then there were Mr. Cabriel and Fr. Ameska, both of whom taught me French at different years. Mr. Cabriel did not speak French, but was excellent at the grammar. Fr. Ameska taught me in my last two years of degree courses. He used to speak French, and we understood him quite well. The Logic classes of Fr. Aleppa were sometimes mind-boggling, but sharpened our thinking. Fr.Doyle was an all-rounder and motivated me to perform better in English. Fr. Sundar, the Principal, was very accessible to students. I was a day scholar, but played football on the college grounds in the evenings, after my classes whenever I didn't have tuition. After playtime, I would shower and go to the international dining hall. All the students from other countries dined there. I enjoyed the company of friends from Singapore, Thailand; and the Middle Eastern Countries. The intercollegiate volleyball tournament hosted by Loyola College was an event that I looked forward to every year. During the last year of my studies, several colleges from nearby states participated in the event. Mar Ivanios College from Trivandrum, Kerala, my home state, had a good team with several players who were good spikes. My support was for this team, even above my own college team. The final match was between Mar Ivanios College and Law College, a local college from the city itself. Mar Ivanios college players resorted to powerful spikes and were in the lead. However, the Law College team understood the poor team-work of their opponents, resorted to intelligent placements and finally won the cup. I cried as if I had become a widow.

I fell sick just a week before the final degree exams. I was diagnosed with gastro-enteritis, which is a water-or food-borne disease. Till the day before exams, I was under treatment. The sickness affected my studies. None the less, I did well in all the exams. Immediately after the exams, I was hospitalized again. This time, I was diagnosed with a duodenal ulcer. After fifteen days in the hospital, I was released, fully recuperated. I went home for my mother's care and waited for the results. My elder brother's marriage was solemnized during my stay at home. His wife was welcomed as a sister by the nine of us. She was a nice person. She looked after the house while our mother was away in the field. She was practically a mother to the last five brothers. Thank God, she understood her job and did it well. We are thankful even today for her valuable service during those years of physical and mental growth.

When the results were published, I had obtained a first class. I wanted to pursue a Master's degree in Chemistry, but it was not one of the choices available at Loyola College. I applied to St. Joseph's College, Trichi, in the same state; and run by the same Jesuit priests, and got selected. After spending two months at home and totally energized, I went to Trichi to continue the studies. I had not seen Trichi before; but had heard a lot about it. The temple built on the rock, known as Rockfort, was a landmark of the city right in the middle of it and was visible from as far as fifty miles. I got a room in the hostel reserved for post-graduate students. Uncle Kurian continued to support me; and my parents borrowed some money from the local bank, by giving their land as guarantee. As I had moved, I had to suspend the tuition business. The course needed total dedication. Twice a week I had lab work that lasted the entire day; the other three days, labs were intermingled with theory classes. The class consisted of just twelve students who were graduates from several colleges spread out all over the state. I was the only one representing Loyola College. Since it was a small class, all of us became close friends rather quickly. Several of the students were orthodox Brahmins, and by custom, strict vegetarians. On those days I had lab the full day, I carried my lunch box and my Brahmin friends were curious as to know what it contained. Some of them hadn't seen the inside of a boiled egg. However, they declined to taste it when I offered it to them.

I climbed the thousand steps to the Hindu temple built on Rockfort a month after I arrived. From up there, one gets a magnificent sight of Trichi and the surrounding places. Many tourists come to Trichi in order to visit the temple. I have visited it several times, each time with more excitement. I also visited the Srirangam and Madurai temples. The Srirangam Temple is a tribute to the art period in which it was constructed. The Madurai Temple, on the other hand, is a marvel of engineering. It has more than six thousand pillars, several of them measuring more than hundred feet tall; they are cut out from a single rock of granite. It is of course with wonder and amazement that one begins to imagine how the pillars, weighing several tones, were hauled to the place and erected with beams of granite equally heavy placed on top of them. The temple was constructed during the administration of three dynasties of kings in Tamil Nadu and has presently been declared as a monument of humanity by the United Nations.

During my studies at St. Joseph's, I had several opportunities to make presentations to my class; and all my classmates gave me excellent feedback. They told me that I was good at oral presentations. I, therefore, felt that my verbal talent was my forte. My effort in developing English in high school was finally paying off. I loved reading, writing and speaking. In spite of majoring in science, I kept reading as many books as I could during my spare times. I believed that my natural talents were related to reading, speaking, and writing, and my calling was in the field of politics, journalism or teaching. Although I did well in chemistry, I felt my talents for quantitative thinking were limited. I graduated with a first class as did half of the class.

After graduation, I had to look for a job to support my family. I also needed to pay back the Brothers who had freely educated me for four years. Uncle Kurian too needed to be paid back. However, I decided to take a small break to visit our relatives in the place from which my family had migrated. My paternal grandfather was still alive. I found him frail, but still walking around. My uncles and cousins were glad to see me and congratulated me on my university degrees. I visited the house of Leela and found her due for delivery. There is a custom that the girl should deliver her first-born in her parents' house. Leela was glad to see me, but I found sadness all over her face. On prodding, she confided to me that her husband drank heavily and that he beat her if she protested. Her husband was from a wealthy family, but a drop-out from school. His father scolded him for squandering the money away with his friends. He had become a parasite and did not commit to anything useful in the family. I felt sad for the fate of Leela and wondered what would be her future. I knew that, if he continued drinking, his health would be affected. I prayed that she wouldn't become a widow with a child to raise.

CHAPTER FIVE

Woodstock and Kent State

The Northwest Orient flight landed in Minneapolis at 7.00 PM, and the pounding of the tires woke me up from my reminiscing. We were met by the Fulbright Orientation Director of the University of Minnesota. Actually, we had arrived late as the program had started two days earlier. We were part of a group of sixty students from all over the world who had come to study in various universities in the US. We three got a quick one-day update program so that we could integrate with the rest of the group. We ate in the dorm cafeteria, and I liked the food. Just imagine the appetite of a young man from India with so much good food in front of him, totally free of cost. I went crazy eating, and my weight went up by ten kilos in one month. I was not worried about the weight gain because I was only forty-five kilos when I left India. The orientation program consisted of talks, workshops, and, visits to different cultural sites in the Minneapolis-Saint Paul area; but what I liked most was the host family weekend program, which consisted of the Fulbright student being hosted by a family during a weekend.

My first host family weekend was very enjoyable. I was picked up on a Saturday at 10 AM by a family from Maryland, but that was vacationing in Brainerd, Minnesota. The husband Mr. Chafee was a PhD in Metallurgy, and the wife was from a well-known rich family in the US. They drove me to their home by the side of a lake. The drive was very picturesque, and the leaves of trees were slowly turning into fall colors. We reached the house, and I was given their son's room to sleep. It was their summer home made entirely of wood. They had venison and wild rice for dinner. I slept like a stone as I was tired, and the temperature was perfect. The next day being Sunday, I accompanied the Chafees for an early morning Mass. They were Catholics. When we returned, Mr. Chafee suggested that he and I swim across the lake in front and have breakfast in the restaurant on the other side. I agreed, not being sure that I could swim all the one mile that seemed the distance. All my previous experience of swimming was limited to small rivers in Kerala. On hind sight, it was too risky a decision. Mrs. Chafee gave me the swimming trunk of her son, and both of us plunged into the water after some black coffee and half a melon each. The water felt cold in July even at 10 in the morning, but soon I got adjusted to the temperature. We were headed for the restaurant, but I noticed that Mrs. Chafee was behind us driving a boat to pick us up in case of need. Seeing her behind gave me confidence and motivation. However, I didn't have the training to swim a mile at a stretch, so I gave up after a quarter of a mile. I waived the sign of tiredness to her, and she came by my side and I got into the boat while Mr. Chafee continued. He too gave up at half-way (perhaps out of consideration for me), and we reached the restaurant. I have never tasted a better breakfast in my whole life; the reason might have been that I really was hungry. We returned to the house and took rest till the afternoon. In the evening, Mr. and Mrs. Chafee drove me to upper Minnesota to watch the fall colors which were more intense in that area. It was spectacular to see both sides of the road filled with trees almost turning into full fall colors of red, yellow, orange and green. I was told that those leaves would fall off as winter approached. I had read and heard about the fall season, but it was the first time I was experiencing it. Mr. and Mrs. Chafee told me that the colors would become even more intense between September and October. It was going to be my first winter, and I was excited about seeing and playing in the snow. We went up to Lake Itasca where the Mississippi river originates. I jumped across the river where it flowed out from the lake.

On the way back, we stopped at a seafood restaurant for dinner by the side of another lake. By the way, Minnesota has more than a thousand lakes. In the restaurant, we could choose the live trout we wanted to eat for dinner. Each of us selected our trout, and it was sent for preparation. Mr. Chafee ordered Champagne, and we did not have to wait for long before the dish arrived. The preparation was amazing and the taste heavenly. It was followed by the special chocolate cake, the favorite of Mrs. Chafee. We returned to the house around 10 PM, and I felt very lucky to have Mr. and Mrs. Chaffee as the host family. I had such a wonderful week-end. They drove me back to the university on Monday morning just on time to get on with the orientation program. I had three more host family experiences, and they were all wonderful, but the Chafees were special. I kept in touch with them for several years, even visiting them in Maryland but losing touch with them eventually.

The first moon landing took place by the Apollo Mission 11 on 20th—July, 1969, and I watched it on a big TV screen. It was an exciting moment when Neil Armstrong pronounced the words, "One small step for a man, and one giant leap for mankind," as he stepped on to the moon's surface. His words echoed into me the thought that my landing on the American continent marked a small step for me, but a giant leap for my family; many followed me to the US eventually. The leap continues even after many years. Later, in 1970, I watched the third moon landing mission, Apollo 13, which was aborted because of an explosion on board and mind-boggling successful effort by the mission control in Houston to get the crew back to earth while the whole of America anxiously waited.

The one-month orientation program went by very fast, and the last day came to say good bye to each other. Perhaps, we would never see each other anymore. The married girl, who came with me, told me that she would bring her husband as soon as she settled down with her studies. Photos of the group were taken, and some autographs were exchanged. I took the flight to Milwaukee and was greeted in the airport by two representatives of the Foreign Students Association of the University of Wisconsin. I was taken to the office of the Foreign Student Advisor, Mrs. Bentley. She was extremely nice to me and assigned me a room in Johnson Hall, where I was to stay during the one-week orientation program. I got introduced to my Faculty Advisor, Dr. Haines, who was the head of the Science and Mathematics Teaching Department. I was the first student from India assigned to him for advice. During our interview, Dr. Hanes observed that all the students from India generally studied science or engineering. He was curious to know why I opted for Education. I told him that although I too was a science student, this was the field in which I could get a Fulbright Grant. I also clarified to Dr. Hanes that Science Education was a subject that interested me. Dr. Haines already knew that I was awarded the Stickney Scholarship from the University of Wisconsin, in addition to the Fulbright Grant. In fact, he was the one who had recommended me for this scholarship. Dr. Haines also added that, depending upon my grades, the scholarship amount could be raised after one year. He was satisfied with my explanations, and we proceeded to select the courses that I would study for the fall semester. Although I had a Master's degree in Chemistry, Dr. Haines thought I should take a course in Chemistry just to refresh my knowledge in the subject since I had graduated two years earlier. I took an inorganic chemistry course which was given at the post-graduate level. Dr. Haines also recommended that I register for three courses in the area of education, an area totally new to me. The courses were selected and registered.

Mrs. Bentley invited me to inform her of the courses I was to take for the semester. She recommended me some housing alternatives for rent. I finally selected the attic of a house which was well furnished. The landlady was kind and very understanding. She gave me the keys and put no restrictions to my coming and going. At the end of the orientation program, I moved into the attic. The landlady had provided facilities for own cooking in the attic, a simple stove, a sink and a few vessels. My mother had taught me to make rice and some Kerala style dishes, but I had decided not to make them out of consideration for the landlady; I was afraid the whole house would smell like curry. I opted to make some western food, but did not know how to cook them. There were no recipes available in those days. I concocted a dish in my head and tried to make it. First, I boiled water and threw some pasta into it. The pasta got over-cooked to the point that it became a soup. I fried some ground beef and condiments and put them into the pasta. What came out was a thick soup which I ate anyway. There was left-over which I ate for the next two meals. The landlady had provided a small refrigerator. Eating out was unthinkable as it cost a lot of money. The cooking got better with time. My biggest problem was loneliness. Even though I was allowed to have friends visit me, I could not stand the loneliness. The confinement feeling of the attic was overwhelming. I moved out after six months into the second floor of a house and got Tony, a Vietnam veteran, to share the rent. Tony worked for the Pabst Blue Ribbon Beer Company and used to bring home beer for the discounted price of two dollars per case. Soon I got into the habit of drinking beer since we had it so ridiculously cheap. By the way, Milwaukee was the beer capital of the US when I was there, home to closely forty brands. Milwaukee had a considerable number of

German immigrants who loved drinking beer, and that explains why so many brands of beer were produced there. Even today, the most popular drink in Germany is beer. When I moved out, all the walls were stacked with empty beer cans.

After one semester and making sure that I earned good grades, Mrs. Bentley allowed me to work part-time. Accordingly, I got a job at Columbia Hospital, which was very conveniently located, just across from the university. I was given a job in the maintenance department. The duties included picking up the trash and arming and disarming special beds for orthopedic patients. From Monday to Friday, I worked four hours per day. On weekends, though, I worked eight hours, sometimes sixteen hours at a stretch. More than once I worked for twenty-four hours. The extra hours were paid double and sometimes triple. My bank account went up, and I had enough money to pay all my debts, especially the loan that I had gotten from Bishop Patroni. I paid uncle Kurian, too. I could even send money home to educate my younger brothers. My companion at work was another student from UWM. He used to consume drugs and showed up at work most of the time under its effects. He used to invite me to go to his apartment after work to smoke a joint. He spoke about Marijuana and LSD, of which I had heard, but never understood their use. I had never used drugs. I always found some excuses not to accompany him. I was afraid of using drugs; I thought it would do harm to my health, that my children would be born deaf or blind. He was a very nice person, but angry with the government for having involved the US in the Vietnam War. Consuming drugs was one way to express the dissent of the student population. There were protests of students against the war in campuses all over the US. The 1969 Woodstock festival took place during my first week in UWM. Woodstock is a small town located in the upper part of New York State. Young people flocked there to listen to loud rock music and consume drugs. This was their style of protest against the politicians that forced them to participate in a war they did not like and the white society that branded them as losers as they refused to conform to its standards. The blacks and minorities too sympathized with and joined the movement. There were Woodstock type festivals all over the US, and I visited one of them not far from the university. During the Vietnam protests in Kent State University in Ohio, on May 4, 1970, four students were shot dead by the National Guards. There were protests in UWM and many campuses all over the US against the massacre. The students at UWM protested with marches, sit-outs, concentrations, speeches and many other activities. I was afraid to go anywhere near the protesters lest I could get shot. I did not have any cause for participation. Once, I was invited by a group of war protesters for a feast. I went to the house where the feast took place. I was accompanied by two of my Indian friends. Everybody was drinking beer. Suddenly I saw the lighted marijuana joint being passed around. I had half a mind to try it just to kill my curiosity for tasting it. Before the joint could reach me, the police broke into the house and started looking for drugs. They searched everywhere, but could not find anything. I did not know where the joint had disappeared. The kids were so adept in dodging the police.

There were other scenes of protests at UWM, this time by the women's liberation movement. Many women students marched through the University halls to protest against the discrimination of women in the society. The men were not at all sympathetic towards this movement. Their comments, as these marches passed by, were hilarious. The hippie and women's liberation movements marked the sixties as revolutionary. The hippie movement sponsored the Woodstock festival. The hippies grew long hairs, dressed informally using mostly torn jeans, played loud music, smoked joints, drank alcohol and broke the codes of sexual conduct as means of protest. The women's liberation movement, on the other hand, sprang up to call attention to the unfair treatment of women in the society in terms of equal rights and opportunities and to support and defend themselves as an organized body. There was a tacit understanding between these two movements to support each other, and most of the time the protests were staged by both movements. The hippie movement had echoes in many parts of the world, especially in cities. During my visit to home after my studies, one of my little brothers received me with long hairs and bell bottom pants. I understood then, how wide the hippie movement was and how it had captured the minds of young people and even children throughout the world. The women's liberation movement did not catch up with the society in India from where I came.

The university life in the US gives one many opportunities to participate in talks by great minds in their subjects. One such talk was given by Professor

Kenneth Galbraith, who was the Ambassador to India during the time of President Kennedy. After the talk, I had the opportunity to meet with him to learn more about the topic of his speech. He presented his latest book, "The New Industrial State". Talks by eminent people were frequent events at the university. The campus was the venue for several rock and roll shows; many cultural activities and dance performances were sponsored by the university. Several movies from all over the world were shown; these were bonuses to the campus life.

I wanted to drive a car because practically all the Americans did drive a car. I took the written test for license and passed it at the first attempt. I called a driving school to give me some practical lessons. A coarse looking lady appeared with her driving school car for practice. On the first day itself, she asked me to drive on the freeway although I thought she overestimated my capacity. After the first lesson, she complimented me for doing so well on the first attempt. After ten lessons, she decided that I was ready to take the test. However, I needed to show up with a car. Since I did not know anyone who would loan me a car, I decided to buy one and take it for the test. I bought an old and odd looking car, a Plymouth Valiant 1962 model, for five hundred dollars. Since it was a standard shift, I had to practice more before I dared to go for the test. The inspector was satisfied with my performance and approved my license there and then. On my way back, it started raining cats and dogs. I could hardly see five feet in front of me. In one intersection, I turned left at the green light without thinking that I had to yield for the incoming traffic. I hit a car, and the traffic stopped. Fortunately, one hour before I went for the test, I had called an insurance agency which had given me a binding. After the accident, I was not sure if the binding would be honored. The police came, did the measurements and worked out the papers. I was given a ticket for a traffic infraction. I went home and called the insurance agency and explained what had happened. The agent who attended told me not to worry and that the company would take care of everything. I paid the infraction ticket and got my car repaired for minor damages. There was no injury to anybody, so the whole thing got resolved without complications.

I was informed from home in India that there was a Fr. Paul, a Catholic priest from my Diocese in Kerala, who was studying in Marquette University in Milwaukee. I located him and found out that the priest knew my family. We became friends and went out together often for pizza and beer. Very soon the priest was joined by his nephew and a neighbor's son, both from Kerala. They were to do post-graduate studies at Marquette. The four of us became very good friends and went everywhere together. Once, we went to Chicago in my car, an hour's drive from Milwaukee, to visit a family known to all of us. On the way back, I was stopped by the Illinois cops for not stopping at a stop sign. I argued with the police that I was a new driver and that I had not really seen the stop sign. The cop asked me a few questions and let me go without a ticket. However, he cautioned me to pay special attention to the road signs and complimented me on my good English. On the freeway back to Milwaukee, another Illinois police vehicle came and blinked the lights on me from behind, but I did not see him as I was looking only in front of me. Besides, I was smoking a cigarette, which we all were, making the car environment suffocating and our eyes watery. As a new driver, I was nervous driving on the freeway, and the cigarette smoke added to the complication. The Illinois police stopped following me as I had already crossed the state line, but called the Wisconsin police to track me down. Soon the Wisconsin police came and blinked the lights from behind me, and I did not see him either. The cop came by my car side and shouted at me through his loud speaker to pull over. I pulled over to the shoulder and came to a stop. The policeman came and asked for the papers, which I promptly produced. "Do you know, why I stopped you?" asked the cop and I said, "I don't know". The cop explained, "I stopped you because you were driving at forty five miles per hour in a lane which is meant for sixty". The cop continued, "I have to give you two tickets, one for driving on the wrong lane for your speed and one not stopping for the Illinois police." I gave all kinds of excuses, including my condition as a new driver and the fact that I was smoking, which I alleged, made me extra cautious. Here, too, I was allowed to go free without a ticket, but with extra advice as to how to drive on freeways. Even to-day I cannot believe how I escaped from tickets in three traffic offenses the same day.

I needed an additional job as my funds had depleted after buying the car. I was told to approach the Dean of the School of Education in order to request a research assistant's job. Accordingly, I requested an interview with the Dean. At the beginning of the interview, the Dean told me that he had only two minutes to hear my case. After two minutes, he told me that I had five more minutes. At the end of the interview, I came away with a job. My initial responsibility was to photocopy articles from journals for the professors. It paid me some badly needed cash, which I sent home to my parents. I still don't know what made the Dean offer me, a foreign student, a job when he could have contracted an American student instead. I will never know the real truth. However, I have a hunch; my attitude made the difference. I was polite, explained coherently why I needed the job and refrained from emotional overtones. The Dean had seen me on several occasions in the library and corridors of the School of Education.

I made friends with the secretaries of the Education Department. One of them was an old lady who invited me for Thanksgiving to her house. Thanksgiving is the most celebrated feast in the US. The origin of the feast is credited to the early settlers from England. They invited the Indians to a feast one day in the year as thanksgiving for having taught them to grow foods like corn, barley and pumpkins. The Indians in turn brought with them turkey, deer and other wild game to roast. Thanksgiving Day was declared as a national feast by the government from America's very early days and is celebrated on the last Thursday of November. The whole family members gather to celebrate and give thanks for the good things they share. The typical dishes include roasted turkey, corn, cranberry sauce and pumpkin pie. The food is served from 3 to 6 PM with a generous portion of alcoholic drinks, followed by a football game which is watched by the entire family. I attended more than one Thanksgiving feast, but the one given by the secretary was the most memorable.

I graduated from the UWM after three semesters and went to Michigan State University (MSU), East Lansing for a PhD degree. I was awarded a Teaching Assistantship at the Science and Mathematics Teaching Center, which helped me pay for the costs. The Teaching Assistantship required that I handled the lab portion of the course Physical Science for Teachers, taught to undergraduate students who were specializing in teaching science in schools. I also tutored students who did not understand certain portions of the lecture. The Teaching Assistantship was an excellent experience because I learnt much about several novel methods of teaching science and mathematics. The semester system in UWM and the quarter system in MSU were faster than the annual system that I was used to in India. Quizzes and exams were administered without previous notice, so there was no time to be complacent. In the beginning, I was caught unawares of the imminence of exams; fortunately, I made up for the time lost. The university library had plenty of books; academic advice was available for the asking. Tutors were available to clear up doubts. The two basic biology courses that my Advisor at MSU had asked me to take were the most difficult. I had to compete with eighteen-year-olds; fresh from the high school, and I had turned thirty-one. They were used to cramming information, and I was at a different level, analyzing and making sense out of them. The grade was determined by the normal curve distribution of scores produced by multiple choice questions. The professor was very skilled at tricking the students with such questions. I just managed to squeeze through both courses, but my brain was very much overheated by cramming. The libraries at both universities where I studied need special mention. The library at UWM was so well set up that one could spend the whole day there. It was open twenty-four hours throughout the year. I spent many nights there. There were comfortable chairs and even blankets to keep one cozy and fall asleep. One could look for as many books as one wanted to read or refer to them. There was a facility for typing one's projects or photocopying pages. I suppose these days there are additional facilities like the internet and other computer-assisted learning resources. The library was well supplied with plenty of books, documents and journals. There was a cafeteria in the basement of the library at UWM if one needed coffee or a quick snack. One could practically live there.

During my studies at MSU, I participated in two conferences, one in New York City and the other in Washington, D.C. At both conferences, I learned a lot by participating in talks, symposiums and exhibits. I even found time to meet some matrimonial prospects from India in those towns, but nothing serious came up. I visited a girl In New York City whom I had known in Milwaukee. She was a practicing doctor in one of the city hospitals. I invited her for lunch, and she agreed. I went to pick her up and had time for a chat. However, when it was time to drive to the restaurant, she backed out saying that she had an emergency to attend. This incident left me doubtful about my capacity to impress girls. I liked another girl I had met in New York. She was a nurse. She told me that she preferred the night duty, and I thought that would hinder our married life. As a result, the case was dropped. After reaching MSU, a priest contacted me and wanted me to meet two of her nieces who were students of nursing in the local university. I met both of them together, but could not make up my mind whom I liked more. The girls probably did not like me either as the priest did not call back. There ended the matter. The drive to New York and back in my car had scary moments as I hardly had one year of driving experience. Fortunately, I was accompanied by one of my African-American friends from Alabama who studied with me. We shared the driving. I found out that one needed quite a bit of previous experience to drive in New York City, especially in Manhattan. On our return, we pulled into a bar for a quick beer in a town called Clear Water in Pennsylvania. It was around 9.00 PM, and there were several folks sitting at the counter. I struck a conversation with a few of them, and one of them asked me if I knew one Mr. Patel, who had worked in their town, in the railways, a few years earlier. I came away admiring the simple folks who live in the country side, for whom the world is a village. We drove the whole night to be on time to teach our classes the next day.

Apart from my Teaching Assistantship, I took up a side job to make some extra money during summer vacations. I worked in the Arlens Department store which was closing down. I worked in the luggage section and was in charge of marking up the prices of items by seventy five percent from the original price. The store then gave a fifty percent discount on the marked-up price. The clients went crazy picking up the items on sale. They were not aware of the original price of an item and got carried away by the generous discount, paying practically the original full price. This is perhaps the story of all sale items. After closing down the store for good, the manager invited me to his house to celebrate the good job we had accomplished. We drank and played pool. When I left at 1.00 AM, I had seven drinks to my credit. I was stopped by a cop in front of the General Motors plant for passing the red light. The workers were getting out after the second shift. I kept a safe distance away from the police. I quietly accepted a traffic ticket and left the place. I could have been in very bad troubles had the cop found out that I was drunk. I still don't know how he neglected to discover it.

I continued taking courses, but my priority was on selecting an area and a topic for the dissertation. The process of selecting a topic and completing a thesis is fraught with many uncertainties. The topic should be a piece in the advancement of knowledge in the subject area, and the Thesis Advisor should be in agreement with the topic and the methodology for its development. I went through one full year of searching for a subject and a topic before I firmly decided upon the thesis. The selection process required a lot of reading and discussion with the Thesis Advisor. Some students change their Advisor several times as they keep changing the topic. My topic interested my Advisor who read through my proposal very carefully and suggested several changes. After several attempts, my proposal was approved, and I was given the green light to proceed with the research. My research work took me to several schools in the State of Michigan. There, I had to convince several science teachers to apply the instrument I had prepared to measure the science interest of their middle school students. I still don't know how I convinced those teachers who usually did not accept intrusions. I distributed among twelve schools one thousand two hundred copies of the instrument and approximately one thousand were filled out and returned. I tabulated the data and performed several statistical analyses using a computer. In those days, the computer occupied two stories of a building and did not have keyboards to introduce the data which had to be punched into a card and fed into a card reader. The print out usually came out after 48 hours. The results were interpreted, and the conclusions were drawn. The whole thing was written up into a thesis consisting of five chapters. The Thesis Advisor supervised all the way until it was presented to the Thesis Committee to read. It took me nearly two years to develop my thesis.

I made several friends from Venezuela, South America, whom I met at Michigan State University. Alejandro was one of them who used to frequent my apartment for casual visits and occasional parties. Alejandro introduced me to a friend of his called Luis. In fact, Luis was in some of my classes, but we did not know each other. Luis also was studying for PhD in Science Education. We both became good friends. I helped out Luis in his thesis preparation by reading through his drafts and making comments. I used to visit Luis's family, and his wife Mia used to prepare excellent Venezuelan food. I too used to prepare Indian food for them. Their three children used to hang on to my neck. Alejandro graduated with a Master's degree in Poultry and went back to Venezuela, and I lost trace of him. Soon Luis too got his PhD degree and went back to Venezuela. However, he returned to the US on business and dropped into my apartment. Luis read through my thesis and made valuable suggestions. He asked me what I was going to do after graduation, and I said I didn't have any clue. Luis invited me to visit Venezuela during the one-month recess during which the thesis was to be read by the Committee. He offered to help me out with the Venezuelan visa. I said I would be delighted to visit Venezuela. South America fascinated me from my school days, especially Brazil and Argentina. I had not heard about Venezuela until I met these friends. From what I heard and the warmth they projected, I imagined that the country must be a fascinating place to visit. Luis went back, and soon I got a call from the Venezuelan Consulate in Chicago to go there and pick up my tourist visa. After making the final touch ups, I submitted the thesis to the Committee for reading. I bought the ticket to Venezuela and went to the Consulate and picked up the visa. The next day, I flew to New York to catch the flight to Caracas, the capital of Venezuela.

CHAPTER SIX

Crossing the Caribbean

I met Alejandro accidentally at the departure terminal in Kennedy Airport after nearly two years of separation. We both were happy to see each other. Alejandro was very happy that I was visiting his country, and I too was excited about it. It was almost a five hours flight to Caracas from JFK. The plane flew down south of the eastern coast of the United States and then crossed the Caribbean Sea to land in Caracas. Although our seats were quite apart, we managed to sit next to each other after the flight took off. We updated each other about all the things that had happened to us during the time of our separation. Alejandro enquired about the purpose of my visit to Venezuela. I told him that I was visiting Luis. I informed him that Luis would be waiting for me at the airport. Luis lived in the town of Maracay, a two hour's drive from the Caracas airport. I had sent him a telegram about the flight details. The VIASA flight crew served us as much champagne as we wanted. It was a government airline, and there were no restrictions to the servings. Everybody was talking, many standing in the aisles. It was like a beehive where people moved constantly. As the plane touched down, all the passengers burst into clapping, which I had never before experienced. I asked Alejandro why people were clapping, and he told me that they were doing it for the pilots for the good landing. They also did this to demonstrate their happiness for returning to their homeland. Even to this day, people still clap as the flights, both domestic and international, touch down at the Venezuelan airports.

After passing through immigration and customs, I looked around for Luis, and he was nowhere to be seen. It was a small airport in those days, and people could easily be located. As I was a total stranger to the country and the Spanish language, I felt disappointed and even a little nervous that Luis was not there to receive me. Alejandro reassured me and suggested that I spent the night in his house in Caracas, a half-hour drive from the airport. He told me that he would drive me to Maracay the next day. His brother had come to pick him up, and we drove to Caracas. As we arrived at around midnight, I was fascinated by the lights on the hills surrounding the city. It was as if the heavens had come down. Alejandro's brother informed him that their sister was already in her house after her delivery in the hospital. We arrived at Alejandro's house, which was located, in a rich neighborhood of Caracas. Alejandro explained my case to his parents, and they were very gracious to receive me into their home. Alejandro took me to the room where I was to sleep and suggested that after a fast bath, I accompany the family to visit the new-born. The sister's house was full of family members celebrating the arrival of the child. I was told that they were celebrating a symbolic ceremony known as the drinking of Miao, meaning urine. Of course, they did not drink urine. The drink was actually a strong alcoholic beverage made of a tropical fruit known as Ponsigue. The drink is traditionally made and buried in the ground when the child is conceived, and the bottles are unearthed on the day of the ceremony. The drink tasted sweet, hot and very strong.

I was introduced to the guests, and I was received with warmth, kindness and friendliness. I felt at ease and gulped a few shots of Miao not knowing the effect it could produce. Alejandro noticed that I was consuming the drink quickly and asked me to take it easy. He explained the treacherous nature of the sweet and smooth drink would eventually hit my head strongly. I took his advice seriously and managed to stay sober. Several people knew English to various degrees of proficiency, and they conversed with me without inhibition. That day, I learned two words in Spanish, 'si' meaning 'yes' and 'no' meaning 'no'. Several types of snacks were served, all of them were very strange to me, but still I tried them all just to oblige the hosts. It is a very a strange world when one ends up in a place with totally different customs and a language that one doesn't understand. I still cannot believe that so many surprises came my way during this journey.

We left the house at around 2 AM, and after grabbing a few slices of pizza on the way, we reached home and slept. I was awakened by Alejandro at 10 AM for breakfast. It was the traditional breakfast menu that consisted of Arepa, which is local bread made of corn, Perico Andino, an egg preparation with onion, tomato, green pepper and black beans sprinkled with local shredded white cheese. The coffee was very concentrated, but very tasty. The best part of the menu was a glass of freshly squeezed orange juice, the taste of which I had never before experienced. No breakfast could have tasted better, I thought. The family enquired about my religion and, knowing that I was Catholic, invited me to accompany them for Sunday Mass at noon. By the way, South America is ninety-six percent Catholic. On the way back, Alejandro told me that we would leave for Maracay as soon as we reached the house. His sister was to accompany us. He proposed that we attend a bullfight in Maracay before we looked for Luis. It was to be a special fight because some famous bullfighters had arrived from Spain for that day. I had heard about bullfighting, but had no idea how it was done. I wondered if I would be near the bull's way but would not voice my concern, lest Alejandro would feel badly and drop the whole idea of going to the fight. In fact, I declared that I had heard a lot about bullfights and was excited to watch one. We reached the stadium around 3 PM and got a seat close to the ring where the fight took place.

In a normal bullfight, each fighter handles two bulls. The stadium was full of spectators. It was a strange experience for me to see a bullfight for the first time; it was both emotional and frightening. The public is separated from the ring by two tall walls with space in between. If the bull jumped at the public, it had to jump the two walls, a feat not easily accomplished by the bull, so the spectators were well protected. The bulls are specially bred for the purpose of fighting just like horses are bred for racing. The bullfight takes place more or less in the following manner: First, the bull is sent into the ring and a few assistant bullfighters play with it showing a red piece of cloth and dodging it, accompanied by shouts of "ole" by the people. Apparently, the bull is very sensitive to the red color and charges at the cloth and not at the fighter. Then the bullfighter gets into the ring and play with the bull with more exciting maneuvers. The people shout "ole" every time the fighter dodges the bull. This will go on for fifteen minutes, and then the bull is pierced with a lance by a man on a horse. The horse is well protected by a thick vest which the bull's horn cannot pierce. The idea of piercing the bull is to make it weaker and fiercer from the pains. Then, between four and eight wooden sticks with sharp metallic ends are planted on the back of the bull to bleed and weaken it further. One can imagine how angry the bull is by this time. Then the bullfighter plays the "ole" with the bull for another fifteen minutes more. When the bull is sufficiently exhausted, it is pierced by a long dagger, and it falls to the ground. If the fighter made the public enjoy the fight, he is awarded one or two ears of the bull like a trophy. The bull is dragged off the ring, and another bull and fighter appear for the next fight.

I got completely jolted out of my seat when I saw the first fighter being taken by the bull horn and thrown off a few yards. I was afraid the fighter wouldn't get up and that he was even dead. To my surprise, the fighter got up quickly, went out of the ring and reappeared to continue with the fight. He had bruises all over his body. He finished the fight, but did not get any ears. The same fighter returned for the fourth bull, and this one was even bigger than the first and seemed more ferocious. The bull trampled him all over, and he was carried off to the clinic. The bull was eventually killed by another fighter. Everybody was talking about how exciting the fights were that day. I wondered how uncivilized a sport it was that injured a bull and then played with it for the pleasure of the spectators. When they were satisfied, they even killed it. It was equally perplexing to see how fighters exposed themselves to being thrown into the air by the bull and carried off with gashing wounds to the nearby hospital. I was told that the bullfighters also die, although only in rare occasions. In fact, one of the most famous bullfighters of Spain, called Pakiri, was killed a few years ago. On the whole, I was happy that I witnessed a bullfight, which was an unexpected bonus of my journey. However, I vowed not to participate in any more fights now that I had seen one.

After the bullfight, we started looking for the house of Luis. We were told that it was close by; indeed it was across the bull ring. When we went to the apartment building where he lived, the concierge told us that he had moved out a week ago to another part of the town. The telegram that I had sent was still in the possession of the concierge. He was unable to deliver it as Luis had left no address. Noticing the disappointment on my face, the concierge added that he had heard Luis saying that he was moving into a housing complex in the eastern part of the city. Maracay in those days was a town of around five hundred thousand people. To locate Luis in this town with just the idea of an area was almost impossible. It was close to seven PM, and I was wondering what I should do, now that Luis was not to be easily located. Understanding my predicament,

Alejandro decided to explore the housing complexes on the east side and ask around for Luis's house. As he drove to the area, I was dealing with the thought that I would have to return to the US empty-handed. Alejandro could not drive around too long as he and his sister had to return to Caracas for work the next day. Caracas was one hour away. As I was mused in my pessimistic thoughts, we stumbled into some boys who were playing in the street. Alejandro stopped the car and asked one of them if he knew Luis Materan. The boy replied that Luis was his Father and that he was upstairs watching TV. The boy shouted, and Luis looked out through the window. I saw Luis and got out from the car and called him down, and Luis was surprised that I had arrived without informing him. One can only imagine the feelings of relief and happiness on my face as I walked into Luis' house. The whole family was there, and they were so happy to see me. After exchanging a few words with Luis and his family, Alejandro and his sister left. Luis told me that he was waiting for news about my arrival. I handed him over the telegram. Mia prepared a sumptuous meal. I slept well thanking God for having helped me to locate Luis. There were indeed many houses in the area and to stumble directly into Luis' house was a miracle; my destiny was made there and then. If I hadn't stumbled into his house, the story of my life would have been totally different, for better or for worse. One small and apparently insignificant incident can change the life history of an individual and all his people. It is an awesome thought that the next step may lead us to an unknown destiny. It is good that we do not think about it all the time for it can make many people paranoid.

The next two days I spent sightseeing, visiting the Teacher's College where Luis worked and meeting with his friends. I felt very comfortable in the company of Luis' friends. They all tried to communicate with me in whatever degree of English they knew. On Tuesday evening, two days into my visit, Luis asked me, "Do you like Venezuela?" I said I loved it, that I was enjoying every bit of my visit, and that I would have enjoyed even more if I had known Spanish. He asked me, "Do you want to work in Venezuela?" I said, "I had never considered that possibility". I asked Luis, "Why are you asking me this question?" He told me, "I thought you were enjoying your visit to Venezuela and that you may consider working in Venezuela after graduation". "My lack of knowledge of Spanish is an impediment", I exclaimed to him. Luis told me, "You will learn it like fish drink water". He offered to call the Ministry of Education in Caracas and request an interview. The next day, Luis told me that the interview was scheduled for Thursday, at 3.00 PM. Since I was leaving on Sunday, everything had to be rushed. On Thursday, we arrived on time in the office of the Director of Higher Education. The Director was a friend of Luis and spoke English well. The interview was very friendly and was over in fifteen minutes, at the end of which the Director offered me a job. I was to work as the Head of Planning of a Community College in Falcon State in the northern end of Venezuela. I had no clue as to where the Community College was located. I was jolted off my seat when the Director told me that the contract would be back dated to the first of the month and that I would get a check corresponding to the first half of the month. I told the Director and Luis that it would be improper for me to accept the money because I could not guarantee returning to Venezuela on time in January; I had just submitted the PhD thesis for review, and there was no guarantee that it would be approved. The Director assured me that he had no doubts that I would get through the thesis at the first attempt. He also added that I could start working whenever the thesis was approved. I could not believe that Venezuelans could be this nice and instantly fell in love with the country and its people. I was handed over a check for the first half of the month of November. The Director even told me that I could pick up the checks for the second half of November and even for the whole month of December when I returned. I was even entitled for a portion of the year-end bonus, added the Director. My mind was blown when I heard this. I was overjoyed to know that I had a job after graduation. I thanked God for finally leading me to a paradise on earth. When Luis cashed the check for me the next day, I could not believe that I was handling so much money, even though it was in the local currency. When I converted it into dollars in the same bank, the amount was a sum that I had never handled as a student. I could not fathom what was happening to me. I wondered if I did well in accepting the job. I argued, however, that if these people were so nice to me and trusted me, I could in turn trust them and their country, too. From this moment onwards I was living a rollercoaster ride between confidence and doubt, about the sanity and stupidity of my decision. What was to happen to my life? What would happen if I could not learn Spanish fast enough? How would I communicate with my family on the other side of the globe? Where would I go if I was fired from the job or if I would quit the job? Which Indian girl would marry me and agree to settle down in Venezuela? Would she learn the language? Would she adjust to the customs and culture of the country? How would I send money to my parents to educate my younger brothers? All these and more questions haunted me, and there was nobody to help me answer them.

I shrugged off these questions and accompanied Luis to Coro where the community college was located. I wanted to have a first-hand look at the institution and the place where I was going to work. It was a four hours drive from Maracay. As we were approaching Coro, the topography indicated that we were passing through a desert-like area. Luis told me that the landmarks of Coro are goats and sand dunes. On the way, one could find goats everywhere. On one side of Coro, there were sand dunes spread out as far as the eyes can see. We arrived at the college building, located at the center of the town. The Director of the institution received us warmly and introduced me to the professors. The Director had been informed of my assignment to his institution by the Ministry of Education, and he was expecting me. The college had been founded by the Ministry of Education six months earlier in a temporary building, formerly a seminary. The Director showed me the site where the new buildings were being constructed. I was not very much impressed by the buildings which were at different stages of completion. They were a far cry from the buildings that I had seen in the US universities. I thought the educational system suffered from lack of a broad vision and that I was precisely there to help them out. It was a mountain of challenge, and I could climb it, I thought. It would take a lot of courage, imagination and hard work to make things better. In any case, there was no going back as I had already accepted the job and even cashed the first paycheck. I did not reveal my inner thoughts to Luis. After the visit to the college, we went around the town which had a history of four hundred years. The oldest part of the town was colonial with stone paved roads and houses with large and tall windows. The people of the town were very proud to exhibit their colonial heritage, and the City Council took very good care to preserve the colonial section of the town. The return journey was uneventful, except that in one of the check posts, my passport was scrutinized by people who looked like they belonged to the military. Luis informed me that they were indeed military belonging to the National Guard, one of the wings of the army, and it was a usual practice in Venezuela that people were stopped, searched and had their identity checked. This was done to catch the illegal immigrants that crossed over to Venezuela from the neighboring countries and catch the drug traffickers. I felt a little uncomfortable with the procedure, may be because it was the first time I was checked by military personnel. I slept that night wondering all that was happening to me, things that I had never imagined in my wildest of dreams. I wondered if I had gone insane by going for a future that was fraught with so much of uncertainty, so wildly different from what I had dreamt. Even the educational system, from the little exposure I had had, looked inadequate and needed much fixing. I would have to tear down many old practices with the risk that my actions would be resented and introduce new ones, which might not be accepted easily. Would I be accepted as the person to do the necessary innovations? Would the local pride stand in the way for a foreigner to come and tell them what to do? Again, I shrugged off these doubts and questions from my mind and fell asleep as I was tired from the journey. Saturday was spent saying goodbye to Luis' friends and shopping, especially for some local products that were not available in the US. I was especially interested in a cowboy hat that I had never before seen. I also bought some indigenous souvenirs for my friends. The flight back on Sunday was scheduled for 3 PM. I had to be at the airport at 12 noon, and so I had to start from the house by 10.30 AM. I accompanied the family for an early Mass on Sunday. After breakfast, Luis suggested that I make a quick visit to the municipal market which was considered a tourist attraction. I said I would go if there was time. Luis asked Mia to pack my suitcase, and we drove to the market. It was busy as Luis had described and very clean in spite of so many people walking around it. One could buy anything and everything one needed, from vegetables, vessels, beef, flowers, handicrafts, to concoctions, you name it. It was different from the supermarket shopping I was used to in the US. We returned to the house and had just enough time to bid goodbye to Mia and the children. Mia told me that she had packed all the clothes that were found in the closet and drawers. Luis loaded the suitcase in the car, and we drove off to the airport. We arrived half an hour late for checking only to find out that the flight was delayed by three hours. PANAM was delayed in Argentina for some unknown reason, and they expected our flight to take off at 9

PM. Luis left me in the airport wishing me well for the return journey. I thanked Luis for all that he had been to me for the last eight days. The moment Luis left, I felt melancholic being alone in the airport, not knowing anyone, being unable to communicate with anyone and uncertain about the future. I had a commitment to return to Venezuela to start working in January, but I had no idea how the thesis defense would go. If I failed, all the plans would be upset for me and for the people in the Ministry of Education. An eventual failure might have meant anything from revising the thesis (which may not be that difficult) to redoing it (which may take any amount of time). What would I do if that happened, even though the Director in the Ministry assured me that he would wait until I finished the thesis? Would the Ministry end up really waiting that long? Should I wait to spend the money until the thesis was successfully completed? How would I give back the money if I ended up never returning? I had plenty of time to roll these questions in my head without finding answers.

As I had too many things to carry in my hand, I put the cowboy hat on my head. The airport vendors were probably seeing for the first time an Indian with a cowboy hat. Several passengers were withdrawing from the flight as it was very much delayed. I got up and walked around to stretch the legs. At 6 PM, PANAM announced that the flight was delayed by another three more hours; now the estimated departure time was midnight and that meant I would reach New York around 5 AM the next day. More passengers started withdrawing from the flight. Hardly around two dozen passengers were left. My flight to Michigan was scheduled for 3 PM the next day, so I didn't have to worry about missing that flight. I was resigned to more waiting. I could not withdraw from the flight as I had to report for work at MSU on Tuesday 8 AM. Besides, I didn't know where to go and spend the night if I withdrew. Caracas was half an hour away in a taxi, and night journey was not recommended. My limitations were clear to me. I preferred to wait for the arrival of the plane. One of those times when I went up and down, I noticed a girl looking at me with special interest. She was sitting along with the other passengers; and hence I guessed that she too was traveling to New York. All the other flights had taken off on time, and ours was the only one left. I couldn't help looking at her once in a while since she was looking at me so insistently. I could not understand why she was looking at me; she even started a shy smile at me. I couldn't muster the courage to return the attention she was showing me. I did not know if she spoke English, but her conduct made me curious and even suspicious. What would she want from me, a total stranger to her? Was she a drug smuggler who would want me to check in one of her bags in my name? Was she going to the US for the first time and needed help? Was she trying to make friends with me? Several answers came to my head, but none of them provided assurance. As I pondered over and over, the plane arrived from Buenos Aires at 11 PM, and the flight was confirmed. I was relieved that I was finally traveling back to New York and that I didn't have to spend the whole night at the airport which was becoming a little cold; I was not carrying a sweater. Finally, we boarded the plane which was nearly empty. In order to facilitate food services, the cabin crew asked the passengers to take seats at the front part of the plane. I moved forward and took a seat and soon noticed the girl had taken a seat close to me. The plane took off, and the cabin crew started serving drinks and food. After food, I decided to muster the courage to talk to her as she seemed still interested in me. I moved to the seat next to her and struck a conversation. She spoke little English—the English that she had learnt in high school. Her English was obviously better than my two words in Spanish, and so the conversation proceeded in English. She made me understand that she was traveling for the first time to the US and that her sister and brother in-law were expected to meet her at the airport. She said that she came from Barcelona, which is located at the eastern part of Venezuela, and that she could not inform her sister in New York or her parents in Barcelona that the flight was reaching the US several hours late. She said that she was not sure that she would find her sister and brother in-law waiting for her at the airport since the flight was so delayed. She carried their address and the telephone number; still she felt very insecure to reach New York at such an odd hour. She said she was afraid of ending up waiting at the airport until her sister came. She even imagined that her sister would never come. I promised her that I would accompany her at the airport until her sister came and would even take her to her sister's apartment by taxi if her sister didn't show up. The address pointed to an apartment located in Bronx. She was quite comforted with my offer. I filled the immigration and customs forms for her. The plane finally touched down around five AM, and it was still very dark in New York, as it was the beginning of the winter season. I stayed behind next to her at the immigration station, and she took some time for clearance. I went through rapidly and met her at the luggage area in order to help her pull out the suitcases. She had two oversized suitcases that seemed to weigh a ton each as I lifted them from the belt. I had a light suitcase which seemed to weigh more than when I took it to Venezuela. I wondered how the few things that I had bought as souvenirs could weigh that much. Again, I stayed back next to her at the customs. All the bags were being checked by the authorities. As her turn came, I moved forward to help her to lift the suitcases for inspection. The customs inspector pulled out several packages of what seemed white powder from the first suitcase. Since the girl did not speak English, the inspector asked me what the packages contained. I said I didn't know either. The custom inspector asked me if I was her husband, and I said no. The Inspector asked me to step behind, kept the packages aside and proceeded to check the second suitcase. He pulled out two packages of banana leaves from it. He again asked me if I knew what it was for. I showed him a bleak face. I whispered to the customs inspector that she was crazy to have brought banana leaves to the US. The inspector called for the agricultural officer, who came and poked the packages that contained the powder and smelled it. She confirmed it was corn flour and let the girl take the packages. She was very curious as to the purpose of the banana leaves. After some hesitation, she let the girl take the leaves, too. I helped her repack and bring down the suitcases, and she continued.

My turn came for inspection. I knew it was going to be fast because I carried nothing declarable. I saw the girl disappearing with her bags on a cart. The customs inspector asked me to open my suitcase and to my surprise, he found three packages of the same powder and one package of banana leaves at the very top. The Inspector asked me why I too was carrying the same things the girl was carrying since I did not know what they were for. I was totally dumbfounded, was at a total loss and started sweating. The Customs Inspector looked at me suspiciously. He, once again asked me if I was sure that the bag belonged to me. The other contents were indeed mine. Again, he asked if I was sure that I was not the girl's husband. I emphatically assured him that I was not her husband. The inspector was at a loss to find an explanation. He looked at my passport once again and checked the data in the customs form. The agricultural officer was nearby to take a look at the findings again. She let me go with the things since she had let the girl go with the same things. I repacked and left the place in a hurry, anxious to know what had happened to the girl. As I walked, I imagined all sorts of things that could have gone wrong with her. If her sister hadn't showed up, I was afraid a New York taxi driver would pressure her to go with him and charge her an exorbitant amount. She also could be in danger as she was a defenseless tourist who didn't speak the language. As I reached the street, the girl waved at me from a moving car which was not a taxi. Thank God she was safe in the company of her sister, I thought. I stood there wondering how the packages of corn powder and banana leaves showed up in my luggage. I suspected Mia who did the final packing for me while I was visiting the municipal market. I searched my bag again and found a note from Mia asking me to give the powder packages, and the banana leaves to Antonio's wife at MSU. Antonio was another friend from Venezuela who was studying for Master's in Civil Engineering. I was too tired to curse Mia for making me go through all the troubles at the customs. I took a taxi to the nearby hotel and fell asleep. I woke up just on time to catch the flight to Detroit. The flight from Detroit to Lansing was short, and Antonio and his family were waiting for me at the airport. I handed over the packages, and they drove me to my apartment. On the way, they explained that the corn flower and the banana leaves were to make a traditional Venezuelan Christmas preparation called hallaca. They invited me to join them for a hallaca night which was to be held the next week. I was happy. After all, my sweating at JFK finally had an explanation and compensation.

There were two weeks left for the defense of the thesis. I read through it several times and prepared the answers for all the imaginable questions that the five professors could ask. Fortunately, my thesis advisor, Dr. Max Berner was very cooperative. He encouraged me to be calm and show confidence. I checked with him all the answers I had prepared for the questions. Dr.Berner read through them and suggested changes. All the questions and their answers were well registered in my brain. The thesis defense took place during the first week of December. There were several questions that I had not anticipated. I answered them as best as I could, and Dr. Berner gave me an encouraging look all the time. Although initially I was sweating, by the end of the defense, I was breathing normally. My gut feeling said that my defense was going well, and that the thesis would be approved. One professor in particular, was asking me several questions, and finally, Dr. Berner took control of the meeting, by telling the group that he thought the thesis was really good and congratulated me on having done a good job in preparing and defending it. He proposed that the thesis be approved, and all were in agreement. Some recommendations for minor changes were made, and I thanked all the professors for reading through my thesis and participating in the defense. I walked out of the room full of joy and gratitude to God. My colleagues, who were waiting outside, were happy that I had passed. All of them congratulated me and recommended that I take a few days of rest. However, I could not afford those few days because I had to make the final changes to the thesis, get it reproduced, bound and distributed to several departments in the university and then head back to Venezuela.

That evening, I went to a Mexican restaurant for dinner. I had enough money to spend, and the mood to celebrate. I ordered the most expensive dish that was on the menu and waited for beer. I reflected how I had just completed the student stage of my life. It hadn't yet sunk into me that I had completed the thesis and that I was a Ph.D. I had come a long way since the day I came to the US three and a half years earlier. It took a long time for the food to arrive because some cooks did not show up for work as there was a blizzard. While I was reminiscing over all the things that had happened to me, my order finally came, and I had already gulped five beers. I had an enormous appetite, and I scooped the spoon right into the middle of the dish which was cooked in earth-ware in an oven (and looked like a stew) and took a mouthful to relish. What I bit was a hot Mexican chilly, and I almost passed out. Seeing the reaction on my face, the waiter came running to me and told that he had forgotten to mention about the chilly. It was too late. I asked for more cold beer to cool the tongue. I waited for a while for the heat to run down and continued with the dish. The chilly flavor added special exquisite to the dish. When I was finished, I had already washed in eight beers, and my head was reeling. I did not feel confident to drive the car back and so went home walking, a three mile distance. Anyway, it was snowing, and driving was not advised. The walk to home was pleasant as I felt that the calories were burning fast to maintain my body temperature. When I arrived at my apartment, the effects of the beers had varied off. The next day, I walked back to look for the car which I had to dig out from two feet of snow.

I called my sponsor NCERT in India and informed them of the completion of my thesis and offered to serve the institution for two years as the Fulbright program demanded. However, the sponsor did not have a job for me at that time and released me from the obligation of returning to India. Such a gesture fitted perfectly into my scheme of returning to Venezuela.

The corrections to the thesis took one week. Sufficient copies were made, and they were distributed to the different departments according to the norms of the university. The degree was to be given at the spring commencement ceremony for which I was not sure to be present. In any case, I was told that my degree would reach me by mail (as it eventually did). I sold off or gave away the little possessions I had and bid goodbye to all my friends and Dr. Berner for all that he had been to me during the years of studies at MSU. I took the flight to New York and stayed two nights with a cousin before flying to Caracas. I bought a Spanish grammar book and an English-Spanish dictionary to learn the language in record time. Now that, I was returning to Venezuela, I decided to learn more about the country. I bought a tourist guide book of Venezuela to read during the flight. The morning PANAM flight to Caracas was uneventful except that the guy next to me showed me a calculator made by Texas Instruments, which was considered a ground-breaking invention at that time. I read that Venezuela is situated north of the equator, bordering Brazil to the south, British Guyana to the east, the Caribbean Sea to the north and Colombia to the west. The Spanish colonizers gave the name Venezuela (little Venice) because it reminded them of Venice. Venezuela won independence from the Spanish colonial rule in 1811 under the leadership of Simon Bolivar, who is considered the Father of the Nation. He helped liberate Colombia, Ecuador, Peru and Bolivia (named after Bolivar), also from their Spanish rulers. The climate is tropical, hot and humid. The world's highest water fall called Angel Falls is located in Venezuela, measuring 2648 feet. The highest and longest cable car in the world is located in the town of Merida on the Andean Mountains of Venezuela. Orinoco River is the largest and most important river of the country.

Petroleum is the major economic activity, accounting for 80% of the country's export earnings. Venezuela is one of the five founding members of OPEC. It used to be an important exporter of coffee and cocoa until the twenties. The national language is Spanish. The three principal races, namely, Spanish,

African and American Indian, have mixed together to produce a healthy and good looking population. No wonder Venezuela has a long tradition of winning beauty contests. I was pleasantly surprised from the first day of my visit that there was absolutely no trace of open racial discrimination in the country. This is perhaps one of the most important reasons why I chose to settle down in Venezuela. It is to be noted that Venezuela was the first country in the world to abolish capital punishment. It has been politically unstable since the time of its independence, ruled mainly by military dictators. However, since 1958, it has enjoyed democratic civilian rule. It has 26 million people with plenty of natural resources. Caracas is the capital of Venezuela, a city with approximately four million people.

As the plane touched down, the usual applause burst out. All the Venezuelans passengers peeped through the windows to identify the relatives that had come to look for them. I too looked through the window and found Luis waiting for me. I gave a sigh of relief as I greeted him outside the terminal. I had crossed the Caribbean Sea to embrace Venezuela as my adopted mother, and she received me with open arms.

CHAPTER SEVEN

Sand Dunes and Goats

Luis drove me to his house in Maracay. On the way, he noticed that a car had crashed into a tree. He stopped and backed up. The driver of the car was thrown out and was bleeding on the ground about fifty feet from the car. We lifted him up, and he was still conscious. We left him in a hospital on the way. What a Good Samaritan Luis was! The next day, we (including Mia and the children) drove to Coro, where I was to stay in a hotel until I found a place to rent. After reserving a room in a hotel, we continued the journey on to Maracaibo, the second biggest city in Venezuela, where Luis and Mia were from. It is a custom in Venezuela that the whole family comes together wherever they are to celebrate Christmas and New Year. I stayed in Luis' house where his Mother, brother and two sisters lived. I was instantly accepted as another member of the family. Everybody was attentive to my needs. I felt bad that I did not speak Spanish, and that they did not speak enough English either; still they tried to speak to me with the broken English they knew. December 24 is a special day in Venezuela. Drinking beer begins early in the morning and continues to next dawn. Food preparations begin in the morning for the celebrations at night. By 10 PM, the table is set with foods, including the traditional hallaca, which I had already tasted in Antonio's house in USA. A lot of fire-crackers are exploded by the people as part of the festivity, especially nearing midnight. All men wear a formal dress, and all the ladies wear a new dress. Everybody visits relatives, friends and neighbors, and everywhere hallaca is served along with other food preparations. Drinks are served generously in every house. Many people go to church to attend the midnight mass, after which, all the members gather around the family table and eat the Christmas dinner. A dancing feast called template is organized by the beer and soft drinks companies at different places in the town. After dinner, the majority of people dance salsa and merengue in the template accompanied by loud music until daybreak, at which time everybody goes back to the house and sleeps. In the evening, people wake up and eat what is left over and do some more visits. The same is repeated at New Year, except that at midnight on the 31st, more fire crackers are exploded. The fireworks by individuals and families practically lit the sky. People visit each other to wish Happy New Year and drive between the firecrackers. Lots of accidents take place on the road because people (with one too many) rush to visit relatives and friends to wish the New Year. Many fire trucks rush to attend emergency calls. The whole place smells of gun powder. Templates are everywhere. As on the twenty-fourth night, the dance lasts till dawn. Everybody is exhausted with so much feasting, and spend the New Year's Day sleeping and resting. Fortunately in Venezuela, the Christmas and New Year vacations last until the Three Magi's day, the 6th of January.

I thanked Luis, his mother, his brother and his sisters for giving me the opportunity to be part of their family to experience the Christmas and New Year celebrations, which were totally new to me. In spite of my limitations with the language, I mingled well with the people. I loved to experience new places, people, and ways of doing things. Luis drove me back to Coro on the 3rd of January. I began to study Spanish and prepare myself for the job. The next day, the director of the community college came to visit me and brought checks for the second half of the month of November, the whole of December, and my portion of the Christmas and yearend bonus. I considered myself the most blessed human being on earth with so much of money for which I did not even work. Then, I sang in my heart the song of King David in Psalm 23, "my cup overflows O Lord".

I wanted to pick up as much Spanish as I could before the college reopened in the second half of January. I buried myself quickly into the grammar book and completed all the eighty lessons in a week. The college was to reopen in a week, and I thought that I should have some firsthand experience in speaking the language. I put the book away and got out into the street to greet people and practice my Spanish. To my great surprise and consternation, I could not utter anything more than the 'si' and the 'no' that I had learned during the previous visit. I thought I had mastered all the grammar and had acquired enough vocabulary to sustain a conversation at least in a limited way. I quickly retired into my room like a dog with its tail between its legs, to escape from the embarrassment and to reflect on what had gone wrong. Obviously my strategy for a quick fix did not work. What other method could I use? Nothing came to my mind. I spent two hours examining all the strategies I could employ, but could not come up with anything practical. I had one of two options: to resign, return the money, and go somewhere else where English is spoken, or to survive in Venezuela at whatever cost. Going somewhere else was not really an option because I did not have a visa to any other country nor a job anywhere else. I could return to India, with the risk of not finding a suitable job that paid enough to meet my responsibilities. I could have gotten married to an Indian nurse in the US (and I knew a few of them who would have done that), got my visa fixed and thereby got my future resolved; but my self-respect did not give into that. I decided to stick it out in Venezuela at whatever cost, but had no clue as to how I would do it. Trying to learn a language in fifteen days for immediate use is not practical; it requires more time. I could not think of starting work without at least a limited use of the language, especially since I was going to be a supervisor with professionals and secretaries that reported to me. After a brief period when my mind was bleak, I thought about a course that I had taken in the University of Wisconsin three years earlier, wherein I was taught how children learned a language. They do not learn grammar or sentence structure. They just listen carefully to what they hear, process it in their mind, and repeat whatever that comes to their mind. I decided I would do just that. I decided to listen carefully to what others said, process it in his mind, make sense out of it, and repeat it in my own way. I made this as my strategy to learn the language. I decided to invite friends to have a beer with me so that I could listen to them and practice with them. Four hours after I retreated from the street, I was back in it inviting friends for a beer. Several friends acceded to my invitation. I listened carefully to all that they said and occasionally uttered something that made sense, but most of the time produced a wink or laughter from them. Although they had a hilarious time at my expense, I did not perceive their behavior as offensive. I felt they were really trying to understand me and give me an opportunity to practice their language. I even perceived that they liked hearing their language badly spoken, because they had never heard it done before. They never transmitted anything that made me feel inhibited. It is a great quality in a culture that facilitates the absorption of people from other latitudes and languages. I felt totally at home and visited the houses of several friends. My efforts paid off, for I began to understand what people said. I even began to utter some sentences, still with errors and accent. I should say that my strategy may not work with everybody who wants to learn a new language. The whole experience that I went through to learn the language sounds easier than what it actually was. Only certain personalities can stand the ordeal surrounding it. First of all, one does not really understand for the first few days what others are saying. One can easily suspect that they are ridiculing him or her. Some may, indeed, laugh at one. One has to develop a thick skin and has the resolve to go forward in spite of all the difficulties. After a few days, it gets better as one begins to understand a little bit more of what is said. Still, the capacity to speak is still further down the road. Until that time, the one who can persist succeeds.

It is pretty scary to end up in a foreign country not knowing the language with the responsibility to do a job that involves supervision of people. One needs one's own family for support, encouragement and as a fallback if things go wrong. I still don't know how I handled the uncertainties and perils associated with my circumstances without emotional breakup. It was adventurous and even crazy on my part. If one thinks about it before being exposed to the real thing, one will never go forward. A friend of mine who started a successful business confessed to me that she would have never started it had she known or reflected over all the perils and challenges that she would have had to face. The secret of any venture is the capacity to face challenges as they come up. That is what I did. Not everybody is born or made for it.

The reopening of the college was postponed by one more week, because the old rented ex-seminary building had to be fumigated. There were some students admitted for basic courses in Math, Spanish and English. The professional curriculum was not yet developed. A number of professors were already hired, but several more were needed. I continued the practice of inviting friends to the bars for conversation and sometimes we went to the beach on weekends and spent the whole day. On the way to the beach, by the side of Coro, one could see, as far as the eyes could perceive, stretches of sand dunes. It is a pleasant sight to see a piece of Sahara desert right in front of one's eye. We used to get down and run into and around sand dunes. Sometimes the sand used to shift places and the road got blocked completely. One had to be very careful driving in these stretches, especially at night. Goats, too, were a normal sight in the arid areas of Coro. Cheese and derivatives made of goat's milk were a local delicacy. After the beach, I was invariably invited to the house of one or another. We entered the house without informing in advance. The ladies never showed any nervousness as I, a total stranger to them, walked into their house. My friend would usually shout, "Mama, pour more water into the soup". I did not understand the saying initially. I thought we were going to have soup for dinner and that she was asked to pour more water into it; but only on a few occasions soup was served. Usually some kind of meat was served with rice and vegetables. Arepa was always present. Later on, I understood that the above saying meant that there was a guest. I always felt welcomed. Foreigners were very much welcomed in Venezuela. A lot of foreigners from Europe came to Venezuela after the Second World War, and they were received with open arms. All of them are well settled and very prosperous. Many foreigners from the other Latin American countries also came to Venezuela during the seventies, eighties and nineties, and they all found livelihood, warmth and help. Even now, people are coming to Venezuela from other Latin American countries and other parts of the world because of the hospitality of the Venezuelans.

I was invited by the director for breakfast on a Sunday, before the college reopened. I got up early and got ready by 7 AM and waited until 9 AM but he did not turn up. At 9.30 AM, I got a call from him saying that something unexpected had come up and so he could not make it. However, he added that we could have lunch together. I skipped breakfast, since the lunch hour was near, and kept waiting. There was no news from the director until 2 PM, when he called again and said that he would be picking me up at 3 PM. I hadn't eaten anything until then. The Director finally turned up at 4 PM and proposed that we just pass by the Radio Club before we went for dinner, now that lunch-time was over. He also mentioned that there were a number of people in the club I would be interested in meeting. I accepted the proposal, thinking that there would be something to eat. When we arrived, a table was reserved for us, and three or four friends of the director were at the table. I could see that they all had a few beers already looking at the number of empty bottles that had accumulated in front of each one. Apparently, the procedure was to settle the bill counting the empty bottles. I was introduced to his friends. More beers were ordered, and I gulped the first bottle at a stretch, as I was very thirsty. The conversation continued, and I was asked some questions about my background. I barely understood the questions and answered them in Spanglish, a Venezuelan term to connote a mixture of English and Spanish. Whenever I was not being understood, the director intervened to explain what I meant. He had studied in the US. The bartender brought ceviche, which is a Peruvian preparation made by curing raw meat or fish in a mixture of vinegar and lime for one full day. Condiments can be added according to taste. The ceviche that was served to us was made from the head of small pigs. I didn't eat pork; I was even allergic to it. Nevertheless, I tasted it to pacify my hunger. I inquired if a sandwich was served in the club, to be told that the canteen was closed on weekends. The director told me that we would leave shortly for dinner. He was not aware that I hadn't eaten anything the whole day. Meanwhile, beer kept coming, and more ceviche was served. Finally we left by 7 PM, and I had seventeen bottles accumulated in front of me. Fortunately, I didn't have to pay for them. Others had more; I had skipped a few rounds. I left several bottles half full as I was conscious that I was drinking on an empty stomach, and that I could get drunk easily. I was already quite drunk, but still on my two feet. The director asked me on the way to the restaurant if I had seen a cockfight. I said I hadn't seen one. The director said there was a cockfight arena outside the town, and on Sunday nights several good fights took place there. He said that we could stop by to watch one fight before we went for dinner. I thought that it was only 7 PM and that we could still go for dinner after watching a fight or two and so I agreed. When we reached the place, there were a number of people betting on the fights that were taking place. We were greeted by a number of the friends of the director. By the way, the director was known to everybody in the town. His family owned the Chevrolet dealership in the town. We sat down between friends to watch the fights. I was introduced to them, and beer was ordered. I suspected that this was going to be long, as I saw a number of cocks in line. Finally, when we left around 10 PM after watching several fights and betting on some of them, I had five more beers in the stomach.

The director drove around, looking for a restaurant that was open. Unfortunately, all were closed or about to close, and none of them admitted clients at that hour. He felt bad and suggested that I request the owner lady of the hotel to prepare some food in her restaurant to get by the night. I agreed, and the director left me at the hotel with twenty two beers in my empty stomach and almost falling. I hadn't eaten anything the whole day except a few pieces of ceviche, which did not reach anywhere. I could not muster sufficient courage to wake up the lady at that odd hour, and so retired to my room. I could not stand the churning in the stomach and so could not sleep at all. Somehow I carried on with my pains until 5 AM, when I went and knocked the door of the hotel lady. The lady opened the door and appeared not very happy that I had interrupted her well-earned sleep. I apologized and explained my problem. She condescended to prepare some food, and asked me to wait in the restaurant. She soon appeared and inquired as to what I wanted to eat. As my Spanish was still not so good to understand the menu, I selected something at random. I had enough hunger to digest even an elephant. She started preparing it in a hurry and brought it on to the table. I knew immediately that I had made the wrong choice, because what I had ordered was pork. She made it rare, as I was in a hurry. I could not eat the food, even with all the hunger I had, because it was pork and half cooked. To make matters worse, the lady sat in front of me at the table as she wanted to clean up and get back to sleep as soon as I had finished. I had to find the means to distract the lady while I threw the pieces of pork for the cat that was waiting under the table. I asked to turn on the TV, and she got busy with a program. I quietly threw the pieces to the cat. I ate the rice and the salad that accompanied the pork. The lady was happy and even surprised that I had finished the food that fast. I was pacified but did not feel satisfied. The next day the cleaning girl told the lady that there were several pieces of pork on the floor. The cat couldn't eat all of them. I had to explain to the lady why I had thrown all the meat to the cat. She claimed that she could have prepared something else if I had informed. I had begun to learn all that people go through when they land in a place where the culture is different, and the language is not understood.

The director informed me that there was a Preschi family, from the US, in town, working in the community college. They came to meet me with their two children. They were from San Jose, California, and had been settled down in Coro for a year. Bobby Preschi's parents were Italian immigrants who had settled down in Venezuela after the Second World War. Bobby was the only son and was born in Venezuela. Bobby's parents used to own and run a restaurant in Coro, which provided them with the funds necessary to send their son to college in the US. Whilst there, Bobby fell in love with Mary Ann, his classmate. Although the parents did not want their son to marry an American, they gave in finally. The marriage took place in Venezuela, but the couple opted to return to the US to continue their studies. The parents, feeling lonely, sold all their properties and returned to Italy. Since they had left Italy for almost forty years, they could not adapt to the life style there either. They returned to Coro and set up another restaurant in a more modest way. The father died of a heart attack, and the mother was left alone. Bobby came back with family and tried to run the restaurant, but his heart was not in the business. His mother, too, followed the father soon after. He sold the restaurant and set up a company to teach English, but the demand for it was not enough for them both to make ends meet. They both were hired to teach English in the community college. I was fascinated by their two children; Rob, who was ten, and Sandy, who was nine. We used to get together very often and spend time together. I was aware that the time spent speaking English in the company of Bobby and Mary Ann was time taken away from Spanish practice, and so I began to limit the time spent with them.

At last, the reopening day of the college came, and I was quite nervous to report for work. I even thought that I should have continued my studies in the US instead of working. I suddenly felt that the carefree student life was better. I shrugged of the nostalgia and reported for work at the director's office at 8 AM. The director hadn't even come to the office. The Preschis warned me that I had to get used to the Venezuelan standard time, which was always 'x' minutes or hours late. It was difficult to adjust to this time management culture after getting used to the American standard time. The director appeared around 9 AM and took me to my office. He introduced me to the secretary and the two engineers who were to work for me. I was given a warm welcome, and several other professors came to greet me. All of them tried to communicate with me with whatever English they could muster. Bobby told me that the two engineers that reported to me could be jealous of me; I was not surprised because I expected it, but I had confidence that I could win them over slowly. Some professors questioned behind my back, how people like me without any connection at the government, and a foreigner at that, without the knowledge of the language, could have been hired as the head of a department. At the end of the day, all of them gave me a break and put up a good face, were respectful, and even warm and friendly. There were moments when the initial euphoria about the first job, the good salary, being in another country, and learning a new language started wearing me out; but whenever that happened, I used to pick up my spirits and deliberately focus on the positive aspects of the job and life. I was getting fifty percent more money than what I would have made, had I been hired to teach in an entry level position, in any of the universities in the US. The extra money was very necessary to educate five of my younger brothers in India. I would have loved to talk to my parents and brothers about my job and life in Venezuela, but there was no way to communicate with them except by letters, which took more than a month to arrive at either side. The Venezuelan postal system was very much underfunded, as very few people used it. Telephone lines did not even exist in the village where I came from. I shrugged off the melancholic moments and got to work earnestly.

The secretary girl was feeling lost, because she did not know how to type anything I wrote in English. I felt bad I could not write in Spanish either. By the way, I was feeling more comfortable with Spanish after two weeks of practice in the field. I could understand more or less what people said, and even made myself understood sometimes. All those beers had paid off. To make things easier, an additional secretary, who was bilingual, was hired for me, and that made a lot of difference. I no longer felt there was a wall between me and the people in the office. Things started running smoothly. The working folks in the college, like the maintenance and security personnel, loved to hear my broken Spanish, and I did not mind speaking with them, because it was an opportunity to practice the language. They were curious as to my customs, especially the ones related to marriage. They wanted to know all about the arranged marriage system, how it worked, and if the married couples were happy. They could not imagine how two people who did not know each other could be happy living together in marriage. Even after, I explained the modern version of arranged marriage; they could not come to terms with it. In their system, courtship duration of five years was the standard before marriage. Occasionally I used to fool them by saying that I had a harem of wives back at home, and they seemed to have believed it. They had heard about harems in the oriental culture. Since I came from the east, they thought I could be practicing polygamy. I even told them that I expected people to respect my traditions if I chose to have local harems. They pointed out that polygamy was prohibited in their Catholic religion. They thought that I could not be a Catholic, as they thought everyone who came from the orient was Hindu or Muslim. When I went to a local store to buy a thermo, the cashier lady told me that she had heard all about me, how I maintained several harems back at home. I had become a notorious person in the town among the common folk.

I bought a used car that belonged to the director. He bought a new one and let me have his Plymouth

Satellite for a fair price. I wrote the exams for the driver's license, and since I did not know Spanish well, I could not understand the written questions; however, the lady that supervised the exams helped me out to mark the right answers in the multiple choice questions. The lady had been contacted earlier by the director to help me out. The practical test was a short drive around the block, and it was easy, as the traffic signals and rules were the same as in the US. I drove the car to work and for pleasure. The car added a lot of mobility to my life.

The community college, at this point, had a number of students. Basic level courses were in progress; but nobody had any idea as to what specialties to offer, and what subjects to teach under each specialty. I quickly got a group of people representing the major industry and commerce within the area of influence of the community college which included practically four states. The most important refineries of the country were located about fifty miles from the college. The refineries participated with full enthusiasm in the meetings. A task force was formed with one representative of each major type of industry and commerce, along with representatives of the professors. The participating companies each assigned one of their personnel full time for a month to work with me to define the specialties to be offered by the college, the curriculum of formation, the contents and the resources required for each course. In the same way, the administrative procedures were set up for admission of students, registration for courses, evaluation of students, and recruitment procedures for professors and staff personnel. We moved into the newly constructed venue in time for specialty courses.

During this period, I met Leoncio Martin, who had also studied at MSU at the same time as I did, but I had never met him there. He came to the college as the representative of the Ministry of Education. We both clicked immediately, and Leo became a colleague and friend of mine. Leo helped me out a lot with the work of the planning department. Without his help, I would not have been able to accomplish the desired results. I bought an IBM computer to help with the registration procedures. By the way, the computer was the first and only one in town. The library was set up with new procedures and books. The day came for the registration of students for the specialties and courses. All went fine, and the college was in full march. I was congratulated by the Ministry of Education, and was invited to be part of the Presidential Commission to organize the founding of a new university. I handed over the administration of the department to my assistants and left for the town of San Cristobal to be sworn in as a member of the said Commission. I spent three months in San Cristobal and finished the research studies that formed the basis for the founding of the university. This university was set up and has been in function for forty five years.

By this time, I had spent one year working for the Ministry and needed a well-deserved vacation. I bought some presents for the folks back at home and took the PANAM flight to New York on the 12th of December. I was flying with Air India for the journey home. The plane broke down in London; and I was stranded for twelve hours. Another plane was arranged to take the passengers to Bombay. It was like a mad house in Bombay. Several passengers had missed connection flights and Air India looked the other way when people complained. Everybody was chasing after any airline personnel that walked by. Finally, after four hours of fighting, I was allotted an air hostess seat in a flight to Madras with the Indian Airlines. The same night I took the train to Calicut. Alian and Lissy lived in the same house from where I had left for the US. The first thing I did in Calicut was to visit Bishop Patroni and thank him for the great favor he did to me. I gave him a present which I had brought from the US, which the bishop appreciated very much. He looked older and still in very good health. This was the last time I would see him, for he died before my next visit.

The next day I went home to visit my parents and brothers. Home coming is the sweetest experience of anyone who has been away abroad. The thatched house was replaced by a new house with the money I had sent. The younger brothers had grown taller and with long hairs. They had acquired a little bit of the hippy culture. The presents were very much appreciated.

After the initial euphoria had died down, the family got into more serious matters. My parents insisted that I get married, since I was thirty-three years old. During my one year bachelorhood in Venezuela, several local girls showed interests in me, but I did not respond to them. Marrying a Venezuelan girl meant any number of years of courtship. I had promised my mother before I left for the US that I would only marry with her approval. I wanted a quick wedding, and that was possible only in India with an arranged type of marriage. I also preferred an Indian girl, a traditional marriage and family alliances. However, I was against dowry. I declared to my parents that

I would not accept dowry, as it was unbecoming to me as an educated person, and against my personal convictions. My parents were taken by surprise by my stance, and my mother argued with me to change my position. Finally, they gave in, and my brother Mohan, who was in the Navy, along with Alian, went into action looking for a suitable bride. Several proposals were discarded as not suitable. Finally, I got married to the daughter of a professor from the college where I had studied. I had known professor Mathai, and he was a very pleasant person to talk to. After my graduation, we had lost touch with each other, until the day I met him accidentally while passing through the town where he lived. Professor Mathai recognized me and enquired about my whereabouts and invited me to his house. There, I was introduced to Melody, his eldest daughter. She attracted my attention, and the next day I called up the professor and requested to visit his family once more, this time with Mohan and Alian. The visit ended up with fixing my marriage with Melody. Her parents, nevertheless, were worried that their daughter was going so far away, where there was nobody known to them. I assuaged their apprehensions, promised that I would look after their daughter the best way possible. Melody and I were married in one week's time, and after one more week of visits to each other's families and relatives, we both took the flight to Delhi en route to New York. I was running out of vacations. In Delhi, the visa to Venezuela for Melody was expedited at the Venezuelan Embassy. Many people wondered if I would ever be able to fix the visa during a passing visit to New Delhi. Some even expected Melody to be back in her parent's house to wait for the visa. I had done some spade work with the Venezuelan Embassy by calling the ambassador as soon as I reached India, alerting the possibility of an eventual marriage. I even bought a few packets of coffee as a present from the ambassador's niece, who was my secretary in Coro. As soon as the marriage was fixed, I called the ambassador and invited her for the marriage. She politely declined, saying that she was committed for that day, but invited me to Delhi with Melody to get the visa stamped into her passport. The visa was issued in one hour. This is the advantage of having contacts and managing relations well to get favors from the Venezuelan authorities. They will gladly bend the rules in order to help you out, provided you approach them with the right attitude.

Melody and I took the PANAM flight to New York. Melody's brother and his foreign wife were waiting to receive us at JFK. The adjustment time for Melody began even from the flight onwards; she could not relish the food that was served in the flight. She was not used to the food without condiments. Melody was seeing her brother after several years. He had left home to the US for studies, but while there, got married secretly to a foreign girl. When the family came to know about the matter, all the members felt terribly sad and betrayed, including Melody. She wondered how she would face her brother and his foreign wife. She wondered what attitude to show towards the sister in law. In the end, she faced them both gracefully. She put up a good face and did not let out her inner feelings in front of them. However, she let her brother know, from some asides, how terribly disappointed the whole family was from his callous behavior. Melody's uncle, whom I had known during our time together in the college, came up from Philadelphia to meet us. The next morning we missed the PANAM flight to Caracas as I fought with the check-in agents for charging me overweight fees for the same amount of luggage I had brought from Delhi without paying any extras. PANAM apologized and put us in the VIASA flight in the evening, but the luggage had already been dispatched in their flight. After reaching Caracas and recuperating the luggage, we went to a hotel and took the early morning flight to Coro. The Preschis had bought a bed set and had taken it to my apartment. They received us in the airport, and thus began our life together in Little Venice.

CHAPTER EIGHT

Home in Little Venice

We wrote letters to our parents informing them of our safe arrival in Venezuela. We could not call them as there was no phone in either of our houses. The letter sent by Melody to her parents took forty-five days to reach them. They panicked and were very much worried as to the fate of their daughter until her letter arrived. Thereafter, they used to get Melody's letters regularly. We settled into the bachelor apartment that I had. The apartment came without a kitchen. For a few days, we ate in the restaurants.

For Melody, everything was a cultural shock. People were not used to seeing women in sari in Venezuela, and so she became a spectacle. She bought some pants and blouses, in which she felt very strange as she was wearing them for the first time. Mary Ann helped her to buy her clothes. She was her counsel and comfort as she could speak to her in English. The food in the restaurants was insipid to Melody's taste as it was generally not spicy. Initially, she did not like the taste of cheese, arepa, bacon and sausage—items that were generally served as part of breakfast. She was not used to eating meat, chicken, pork or fish without curry. We quickly fixed the kitchen, but could not get Indian style curry powder anywhere. The curry powder bought in the local supermarket did not quite taste authentically Indian. However, Melody felt much better now that she was able to cook.

Settling down in another country was a constant process of learning and adjustment for Melody, fresh off the boat. She had to learn the language, and I took up the task of teaching her. Since I did not believe in learning the grammar as the route to learning the language, I taught her the basics in small bits from the book and asked her to get into the street and practice speaking with the common folks, like the waiters in the cafeteria, the people in the fish or meat shop, the sales lady in the department store or the girl in the neighbor's house. However, my formula did not work as Melody's personality was different from mine; she was too shy to strike and maintain a conversation with people not well known to her, especially men. As a result, she continued learning the language at a slow pace. Also, we were invited for feasts in the house of friends for birthdays, weddings, baptisms, first communions and other important events. Venezuelans loved to feast. It was their way of relaxing and getting the stress out of their system. I have never met another group of people who has a better capacity to enjoy life. Their motto was; "enjoy today and tomorrow will take care of itself". The feasts invariably ended up in dance. The Venezuelans, and for that matter the Latin Americans, are good at dancing. They have several rhythms: salsa, merengue, cumbia, boleros, cha cha and many more. During the feasts, everybody gets to the dance floor at the beckoning of appropriate music. People expected Melody and me to dance, but we dared not try it as we were unable to perform like the locals. To see the steps, twists and flows of Venezuelans were a joy, but we didn't even know the basic steps, let alone able to dance like them. Hence, we were inhibited from getting on to the dance floor and, so, stayed as onlookers. We felt a little isolated and would leave the feast earlier than others. Also, there are no taboos for social mixing between men and women. They are of equal footing in the society and treat each other on this premise. They invite each other, even if they are strangers, to social dancing. The girls even invite married men and vice versa. These are practices which were foreign to the Indian customs, and we had to learn to deal with them and even accept them.

I took Melody to my office to introduce her to colleagues and friends. The men were very happy to see an Indian girl, most of them for the first time. Some secretaries and lady professors did not like that I had gone to India to look for a wife; they even hinted that I had hidden the fact that I had had a girl-friend back at home. They could not believe my story that I got married after knowing Melody only for a few hours. Some girls even went so far as to suggest that Melody was one of my harems, that I did not like Venezuelan girls. However, in the end, we were accepted and welcomed in the college community.

One Sunday, after Mass, I took Melody to Don Camilo, a restaurant well known in Coro, for lunch. I wanted to show her how good the restaurant was as I had eaten several times there. After ordering a turtle soup as a starter for her, which was considered a delicacy, I asked the waiter to suggest something different for me. The waiter suggested a new item called the Caribbean Crab, which I ordered not knowing what exactly it was. I was not afraid of the unknown. While the food was being prepared, I had a few beers. The starters came, and Melody began to enjoy her soup. The crab was big, whole, and steaming hot. The waiter looked at me to see how I was going to handle it. I was totally at a loss as to what to do with it. The waiter then told me that he had forgotten the nut cracker to open the crab, and he went and brought it. Even then I did not know how to eat the crab. People on the other tables were looking at me from the corner of their eyes, and Melody kept waiting for me to do something with the crab. I waited for some time thinking what to do. In order not to look like a fool in front of the entire audience, I put the crab between the handles of the nut cracker and pressed. The whole creamy hot crab meat splashed on to my face. I wiped my face clean with the napkin and went to wash. I was afraid I had burnt my face and would end up with scars. Nobody wanted to look at me as I returned from the wash room since they were unsure they could hold their laughter. I asked the waiter to remove the disfigured crab and waited for the entree. The unknown can be sometimes baffling and even dangerous. This is the lesson that I learnt that day. Adventure is my second nature and once in a while I pay for risk taking. I would not have ended up in Venezuela if I had not been a risk taker. On the whole, my score card is positive.

When I was away in India, the presidential elections were conducted in Venezuela, and the opposition leader won with a landslide victory. Even though, it is hard to believe, the change of government in Venezuela affects even secretaries. Once the change takes place, all or most of the employees, who held government jobs from the party that lost, are replaced by members of the party that won. It is like winning a war and dividing the spoils of the olden days. Thus, I was sad to see the Director leave his job to go into private practice. I even saw the secretary of the Director being replaced by another that belonged to the party that won. Most, if not all the recruitment for jobs in college, was based on party affiliation. I was so shocked to notice that for the election of the office bearers of the Association of Professors, the competing groups were formed strictly on party affiliation.

I was invited by the British Embassy in Caracas to participate in the Industrial Trade Fair that was held in Sao Paulo, Brazil. I left Melody in the house of Leo in Maracay and joined the delegation from Venezuela. Although Portuguese is the language of Brazil, I could understand it quite well as I had a good command of Spanish. I was invited to the fair to see the lab equipment and chemicals that were produced by the British companies. I had ordered several items from them for the community college. When I returned after one week, I picked up Melody from Leo's house. I had parked the car on the street in front of Leo's house, and it was on a slope. I put the automatic gear to neutral before starting the engine, and the car started rolling down backward. I applied the brake, but it wouldn't work. When I looked behind, I saw several children playing down the street. I turned the steering with all my strength to one side. The car turned around before it could hit the children, and the back wheels hit against the curve, and I managed to stop it. Everything happened so fast that Melody, who was inside the car, did not even understand what was happening. Leo and his Father were seeing what was happening, but they were helpless onlookers. As the car came to a halt, they came running to inquire what had happened. We all learned that cars with automatic gears do not catch breaks unless the engine is started. The modern cars do not allow shifting from the park without starting. Once we got over the shock, we started back to Coro. Knowing that we couldn't reach before dark, we stayed in a hotel for the night. At dinner, Melody told me the happy news that she was expecting. The doctor checked her in Coro and confirmed the good news. They said that everything was normal with her.

Meanwhile, Leo was arranging for my transfer to the Teachers' College in Maracay. This institution was founded by the Ministry of Education to prepare students as professional teachers. It had a five year curriculum of studies. The Teachers' College had been in function for two years offering only the basic courses. The professional curriculum was yet to be designed and developed. The idea of my transfer to the Teachers' College was for me to be part of the team that would develop the curriculum and the courses. I finally got transferred to Maracay in the month of October. Our stay in Coro lasted only eight months. When I arrived, my friend Luis was no longer there; he had been transferred to another institution in the town of

Barquisimeto. We bought an apartment in a building near the Teachers' College, and I started working earnestly. I designed several courses for teachers training and even taught some of them.

When Melody was eight months pregnant, an earth-quake of medium magnitude occurred while she was in the apartment on the 14th floor. At this height, even a moderate quake is very much felt. She was experiencing the quake for the first time and was very frightened, especially because she was alone. "The whole building seemed to swing and sway", she said. I went running, but she was already on the ground floor. She came down the stairs slowly, and some neighbors helped her out. She was very much shaken. I took her for a last check-up before delivery. I noticed her stomach was unusually big and asked the doctor if there were twins. The doctor's reply was hilarious; "I don't know if you have any on the sides, but here there is only one". The question was legitimate as the ultrasound technology was not yet developed, but his answer was better still, typical of Venezuelan humor. Melody broke her fluid membrane one day early in the morning, and I rushed her to the hospital. The pain slowly started and increased in frequency and intensity. I kept company with her and rubbed her back, but whom she needed most at that time was her mother or one of her sisters. The doctor once in a while came, checked the dilation and went away. One nurse told her that she had delivered four times and every time the pain was more excruciating. That was not any consolation. Another nurse brought a piece of cloth for Melody to bite at the peak of the pain. At last, she was taken to the delivery room around 4 PM. None of our friends had arrived yet. I bought a packet of cigarettes and smoked away the waiting hours. Men were not allowed into the delivery room in those days. At last at 6.15 PM, I saw the nurses running around. One of them told me that it was a girl. I waited for somebody to call me into the delivery room. At last the doctor came and asked me to follow him. I sensed there was something wrong. We went into an office nearby, and the doctor told me that the baby had died without breathing. She has been alive when she was born, but in spite of being slapped several times, she did not breathe. The doctor told me that he did everything possible to revive the child, but it was of no avail. He also told me that he would get an autopsy done and let me know the results. The doctor led me to the room where the child was kept. I looked at my daughter and thought she was very beautiful. I contemplated for a while her beautiful face, but held my tears in front of the doctor and the nurse. Then I was led to the room where Melody was. We both wept a lot, and we were left alone. There was nobody to share our grief. The Kirthys, a couple from India, arrived after a while and consoled us. The Prakashes, another Indian family, arrived later at night and comforted us. The night was for us without moon or stars. The next day was 19th April, a day of national feasting in Venezuela. Our friends from the Teachers' College, Eduardo and his wife Karina came to keep us company and made all the arrangements for the burial of our child. Leo also came to inquire about what had happened. Karina called a priest to baptize our daughter and called her Annie. We buried her in the municipal cemetery, and I came back with a cross taken from the coffin, feeling that I had left a part of me there.

Melody was discharged the next day, and we went home empty-handed. She could not hold her tears whenever she saw the clothes, the dresses and the crib we had bought. We felt our life had been shattered. We feared for a future without children, and that was beyond what we could bear. We gave all the items away that we had bought for the baby, just not to be reminded of the tragedy.

Eduardo introduced us to a Dr. Carlos Pantin who lived nearby. He came and assured us that what had happened to us was just an accident and that the probability of repeating it was very low. He recommended that we both get checked out in a research institute located near Caracas to discard any genetic problem before we went for another child. Accordingly, we went to the institute that Dr. Pantin recommended. The doctors thoroughly checked us out and declared us healthy to go forward and try for another child. We slowly left behind the tragedy and carried on with our lives. Dr.Pantin was a practitioner who believed in regular exercises. He used to get up at 5 AM and run three kilometers. He asked me to join him and his other friends, which I did and have continued the practice for many years.

My work of course design and teaching continued at the Teachers' College. In the Educational Statistics course that I taught, there was a person called Guillermo Prince from Uruguay. He was well built, studious and friendly. I used to give him a ride after class. One day, a lady knocked at the door of my apartment, and I reluctantly opened it. She introduced herself as a sales lady for Encyclopedia Britannica. I usually didn't allow sales people to get further than the introductory stage. However, her introductory pitch was so good that I asked her to enter. Her name was Carolina, and I found out that she was the wife of Guillermo and that they had a boy aged ten-years. I did not buy the encyclopedia, but Carolina was happy that she met Melody and me. One week after our meeting, she came again, this time sobbing. I inquired about her problem, and she explained that her husband had one swollen testicle. I arranged for Guillermo to see a doctor who removed the swollen testicle. A piece of it was sent for biopsy. I still don't know why the doctor removed the testicle without allowing the patient to have a second opinion. Maybe he was greedy for money. However, the biopsy result came out positive. The family did not have enough means to get proper treatment. Meanwhile, the other testicle also became swollen. The family became very depressed. There was a right mixture for a tragedy to happen. I talked to some friends, and none of them could come up with a solution. Then a lady belonging to an Evangelical group approached me and told me that there was a non-conventional treatment for cancer in Mexico. The treatment consisted of electric acupuncture. There was a doctor in the nearby town who knew about it. I took Guillermo to see this doctor who recommended that he went to Mexico for three months treatment. The Evangelical church offered to pay for the costs of the ticket. Guillermo could scramble from his own pocket money payment for the treatment and living expenses. All their savings were to be used, and there was no money left for his wife and child to live on. I talked with the Director of the Teachers College, and he offered to hire Carolina as a secretary. She did not know typing or have any experience as a secretary. She did her best and appreciated the break that was given to her. Guillermo was on his way to Mexico. There was one more person who was traveling with him who suffered from liver cancer. Between the two, they took an apartment for rent for three months in Mexico City. During the first week, the other companion died. That made Guillermo panicky, and he wanted to return to die at home in the company of his wife and son. I called him and insisted that he finished the treatment and encouraged his wife to recommend him to do so. When he left the clinic after three months, the doctors declared him cancer free. He did not believe it. He came back and submitted to another biopsy which came out negative. The family was happy finally. However, within two months, his wife came running to Melody telling her that she was pregnant and that she was afraid the child wouldn't be healthy. Melody consoled her saying that everything was going to be all right. Nine months later, they hugged their healthy beautiful daughter. Who can understand the ways of God?

Another incident also occurred about the same time. There was a Colombian family living on the 13th floor of the building, just one floor below ours. They had two grown up boys. The younger one appeared to suffer from some illness, which we could not figure out what it was. He was moody and a loner. One day, when I was standing on my balcony, I saw the boy going through the balcony below and falling on the roof of the parking lot with a loud noise. I dashed through the door and went down the stairs. I was the first one to reach the scene and found the boy standing up. The parents also reached him, as did several neighbors. The boy was not harmed as he had landed on one side of the aluminum roof which bent down to the floor. The roof had collapsed. The boy was taken to the hospital for minor cuts and bruises and was discharged the same day. The parents told me later that he was suffering from a mental illness.

Another Indian family, the Devans joined our group. They were from the same state where we came from and, so we spoke the same language. Devan was a specialist in food production and was advising a local food processing company. Sarala was a housewife who used to prepare the most delicious dishes. They were excellent hosts and enjoyed visitors in their house. All the local expatriates from India used to meet in their house during weekends to eat Sarala's food and play cards. Soon Devan brought Raghavan, an engineer, the son of his late friend in Nigeria who had died in a traffic accident. Ravi was a mechanical engineer who had found a job as a maintenance engineer for a sugar company in the eastern part of Venezuela. He used to visit the Devans on some weekends and join the group in the card games.

Melody was pregnant again, and this time I took extra precautions, with periodic check-ups with another doctor throughout her nine months. There was nothing unusual during the whole pregnancy. She started feeling pains one evening, and I rushed her to the hospital where her doctor worked. Her doctor declared· that she was in labor. The child was born the next day at 11 AM, a healthy girl. We named her Roshni. All our friends came to share in our joy. The next morning the pediatrician found the baby turning yellow. Then her doctor found out that Melody and I were incompatible blood types. Melody was O+, and I was A+, and the child came out as A+. O blood type can receive only O type blood and rejects and even fights with other blood types like A, B and AB. Since our child's A blood had gotten mixed with Melody's O blood during gestation, a substance known as bilirubin had been produced in Melody's body. This substance had passed to our child's body, giving her a yellow tone. The child was exposed to flood lights as treatment. If the bilirubin concentration had increased to more than twenty units, it could have affected the brain of the child. The initial reading showed eight units, the second thirteen units, and the third showed ten units, which meant the problem was getting resolved. However, when the pediatrician came and checked the child in the evening on the third day, she appeared more yellow. The pediatrician decided to test the blood in a different lab, and the result came out as nineteen units, which meant that our daughter was entering into a critical stage. The doctors immediately decided to do a blood transfusion on Roshni. I called Dr. Pantin, and he came running. He called a blood specialist who took charge of the transfusion. Raghavan was the one who accompanied me. We waited on the cold benches of the clinic for the procedure to be completed. It was 2 AM, and the doctors announced that everything had gone well. Roshni continued to be placed under flood light and recuperated in two days. We went home with instruction from the doctors to expose her to sun-light for half an hour every day for one week. Roshni recuperated completely, and we felt that the angel that had flown away had returned. During the first visit, the pediatrician told us that the lab at the clinic had been 'cooking up' the results without really doing the tests.

Roshni filled an enormous vacuum in our life. She took away our sadness, our loneliness and compensated somewhat for the loss of Annie. Life was no more the same as before. Initially we were clumsy preparing the formula, changing diapers, bathing, changing dress, feeding and taking out the gas and putting Roshni to sleep, but we became better at them as time went on. We changed her diet as prescribed by the pediatrician. We gave her all the shots on time. We walked her in the stroller around the parks and shopping centers. Once, she jumped headlong from the stroller to catch a doll that had fallen. I caught her on time and avoided a tragedy. We took plenty of photos, made an album and sent a few of them home. We finally felt realized our blessings and thanked God every day for the greatest gift to which a couple can aspire. After five, months, Sarala too delivered a child, a good looking boy, and named him Ashok. The joy in the Indian community was doubled by the arrival of the new baby boy. Roshni stood out as the only baby girl among the Indian community.

When Roshni was six months old, we decided to baptize her, and we selected Eduardo and Karina as God parents. Among the Indian friends, there were none who were Catholic to be named as God parent. We invited all our close friends. Roshni was given the Baptismal name Ann. We have a tradition to give the first born girl the baptismal name of the paternal grandmother. In this case, both the grandmothers had the same name. After the ceremony, we went to our apartment and celebrated in grand style. We had ordered Paella, which is a well known dish in all Latin American countries and Spain. There was plenty left over, and everybody took home as much as each wanted. Leo too came for the baptism. He intimated to me that he was leaving the Teachers' College to take up a job with a social foundation called Fudeco in Barquisimeto. Now Fudeco was a well known institution in Venezuela for social projects. It had started an educational projects division and wanted someone to head it. The position was offered to Leo, and he accepted it. As a result, he was leaving the Teachers' Colleges. I wished him good luck. I thought I was not going to see him frequently. However, within a week Leo was standing in front of my door to ask me if I would join him at Fudeco. It was an offer to which I couldn't say no because of our friendship. I went through interviews and was offered the job, and I accepted it. I went to Barquisimeto with Melody and Roshni to look around for a house to rent, but found a good deal to buy an apartment. I reserved it and came back to Maracay to sell our apartment. With the money we got, we made the down payment for two apartments: one in Barquisimeto and another in Maracay itself. This last apartment was rented out, and we moved to Barquisimeto. The apartment we bought in Barquisimeto was close enough that I could walk to work. We liked the new apartment and made friends with the neighbors on the same floor. The neighbor couple had a boy of the age of Roshni, and they both were good company to each other.

We had not gone home to India since our arrival after our marriage three years earlier, and a visit to home was overdue. However, when one is just one month into a new job, one doesn't ask for vacation. I discussed the matter with Leo, and he approved the journey on grounds that it was going to be more difficult to take a vacation once the projects started earnestly. We were elated that we could go home and bought many presents. We took the PANAM flight to New York and stayed in a hotel in Manhattan. We bought more presents and left for Bombay by PANAM the day after. The flight made a stop in Karachi, where the first thing many incoming passengers rushed for was beer. They grabbed as many cans as they could find. They would start drinking right away, even before the plane departed. The air hostesses had a hard time keeping control of them. My brother Mohan was waiting for us at the airport. Mohan accompanied us to the flight to Madras and then on to Cochin the next day. My Father and a few of my brothers were there to receive us along with Melody's parents. After resting for a while in a hotel, we took the overnight train to my house. Two days later, we made the same journey back and went to Melody's house. Her parents had contracted a girl to look after Roshni. The girl did a superb job of looking after the child, and she was asked to stay in Melody's home as she was an orphan and deaf. Even to-day she is with the family looking after the needs of all.

Before I could realize that I was on vacation, it was over. It was practically spent on trains traveling back and forth the two houses. The heat and rain, the smell and dirt, the crowd and pickpockets, the archaic procedures and late arrivals all made the travel nerve wrecking. I was totally exhausted when I boarded the return flight. Melody and Roshni were left behind to enjoy a few more days of vacation. On arrival at New

York, I checked into a hotel for the night. The next day, I could not get up as my head was reeling, and continued to sleep. When I woke up after twenty-four hours, I had missed the flight to Caracas. Fortunately, I got a reservation for the next day's flight. I called Leo and explained what had happened. I reported for duty one day late and had to catch up with the schedule of completion of projects. Catch up I did; I was alone and could dedicate all my efforts and time for the work.

CHAPTER NINE

Dancing the Tamunangue

I got a letter from Melody, hand-carried and posted in New York. In it, she said that not long after I left, Roshni contracted gastroenteritis and was hospitalized. She said that after three days in the hospital, the child had lost a lot of weight. I was saddened to know that Roshni, who had a healthy look, had lost it. When she came back, she was feather light. We took care of her, and slowly, she came back to her original weight. She talked like a bird, and nobody could understand what she said. At fourteen months, she could not walk. We would stand her on her feet and leave her to walk, but she would sit down. We were worried that she was not showing the developments other children her age were showing. But, one day in her sixteenth month, she just got up by herself, walked a little bit and then ran. At last, she found out that she could not only walk but run. From this behavior, I concluded that her types of personality need a sufficient guarantee of success before attempting something risky. She carried this trait even into adulthood. Twenty years later, she wouldn't attempt to drive on the freeway as a new driver. However much I forced her to get on the freeway, she wouldn't do it. After driving for a while, from home to college and back, she tried driving on the free-way a few times and found she could do it. Now, she is an expert at driving on any road. I looked for an end result and didn't care for the process. It is a process of development. Each child or adult takes their own time to go through the process. If one realizes this fact, one can enjoy the process. If not, one is doomed to be disappointed.

Not too long after she returned from India, Melody was again with child. This time, we wanted to make sure that the blood incompatibility problem would be better taken care of. We approached the best lady doctor in the town to monitor the pregnancy. The doctor decided to carry out periodic tests of bilirubin content in the mother's blood. The tests showed that the child's blood was A+, just as Roshni's, and so there was going to be blood incompatibility. The bilirubin reading started at eight units, and went all the way up to fourteen. The doctor decided to induce labor at the 32nd week of gestation, eight weeks short of the normal pregnancy period. A baby boy was born, and we named him Rajeev. He was placed in the incubator and treated with flood lights. The tests for bilirubin showed that it was increasing, and so the doctors prepared for a blood transfusion. But the subsequent tests showed that it was diminishing, and, so, the transfusion procedure was abandoned. We took the child home after two days, and exposed him to sun rays twice a day for half an hour, according to the doctor's instructions. Within a week, he recuperated.

The arrival of the second child, not too far apart from the first, made Melody's life a little difficult. We contracted a nanny to help out with the children. The nanny initially took care of Roshni so that she would not get in the way of the mother and the baby. She did not like the idea at all; she wanted to be part of the show all the time. The nanny spoke Spanish to her, and so she switched from English to Spanish. Before long, it became her mother tongue. Rajeev had a problem with retaining milk. He used to drink a full bottle, but would vomit it out at the slightest discomfort. This meant feeding him again. We took him to the pediatrician to find a solution to the problem. The pediatrician told us that some children, especially boys, suffered from this problem, and that they usually got over it around the age of two. There was no solution other than to wait until then. There was no place in the apartment where he hadn't vomited. Fortunately, the day he completed two years, he stopped vomiting and the problem never recurred. The doctor was right on the money.

It was time to get Roshni into pre-kinder, and we found a small but good school around the area where we lived. She was admitted there and was happy to go to school and play with her friends. A special type of dance known as thamunangue, whose origin is in Barquisimeto, was taught in the school for all the girls. Six months into the school year, a thamunangue dance program, was arranged for all the girls in Roshni's class, as part of the year-end school celebration. The teacher told me that Roshni was very good at it and that she would be included in the performance. I took her to the dance practice without fail so that she could become perfect at it. On the day of the performance, she was put in front so that all could watch and enjoy her dance. I loaded my camera and sat in the first row so that I could take the best pictures. The dance program started, and Roshni's class came fifth in the line. I took a few pictures of the other programs but reserved most of the shots for Roshni's. Her class came on the stage, and she was right in front. She saw me and smiled a little bit and turned her eyes away. The music started and all the children started dancing except Roshni. She stayed looking down, immovable, with both her hands folded, the whole time the dance was going on. The teacher looked at me in disbelief. I was very disappointed that all my efforts to take pictures went to waste. After the dance, she came and sat by my side, and I asked her why she didn't dance. She said she did not dance because I was looking at her. Who understands children's psychology? At the age of thirty, when she was exercising with a CD, I walked into the scene, and she stopped doing the exercise. I asked her why she stopped, and she replied, "because you are looking at me". This is a personality issue. Can personality be changed? Apparently not, and Roshni is the proof.

When Rajeev was nine months old, we were happy to know that we were going to be parents of one more child. All the precautions were put in place. In the third month, we found out that the child had the same blood as her mother's, and, so, there was not going to be any incompatibility problem. We thanked God for this good news and continued with our daily routines. We went on a trip to the US, visited our family members in Chicago, and then proceeded to Cleveland in Ohio, where Melody's uncle lived. Melody's grandfather was visiting the uncle.

The grandfather was very happy to see his two great grandchildren from Venezuela. We decided to get Rajeev baptized in the local church. Melody's brother came from Chicago to be the godfather. The aunt in Cleveland became the godmother. The ceremony was followed by a lunch for all the guests in a boat club. Melody, five months pregnant, handled the ceremony and the feast without showing much strain. A marriage proposal was discussed for the younger sister of the uncle, that is, Melody's aunt who was in India. The proposed young man was visiting the uncle's house. The uncle quietly asked me to scrutinize his educational qualifications. I asked him a few questions regarding where he had studied and details about the subjects. He seemed contradictory and nervous. At one point, I decided to call the universities where he said he had studied and found out that he hadn't even stepped into those institutions. He became suspicious about my questioning and suddenly decided to leave, giving some silly excuses. After he left, I disclosed to the family what I had found out about him, and the uncle thanked me for saving his sister from getting married to that cheat and liar.

I was involved in several projects, on behalf of Fudeco, with one of the refineries of the Venezuelan Petroleum Company (VPC). One of the projects was a task analysis of some jobs. There were more than seventy positions to be described in terms of the tasks performed, and the knowledge, skill, and attitude required for each task. This was to be followed by the evaluation of the employee in the performance of the tasks. Based on deficiencies of knowledge, skills, and attitude, training programs were prescribed. This was an enormous job and required the participation of several professionals. The refinery facilitated most of these professionals, and the data-base was constructed by my team. The task analysis alone took six months. One day, when I was in the refinery, Melody entered into labor pains, and the neighbor rushed her to the hospital. I drove back and was on time for the delivery. Roshni and Rajeev were under the care of the nanny at home. The child was born without complications, and we named her Ranya. Our greatest blessing in life is the RRR: Roshni, Rajeev, and Ranya. We had our hands full with three small children. The nanny too, was very busy with the two older ones. We hired a second nanny to take care of Ranya and to take care of the kitchen, as Melody was recommended bed rest for a month. I was gone from Monday to Friday to the refinery, and that complicated matters a lot for Melody. We pulled through the first month after the delivery, and the second nanny was terminated, and life more or less settled to normality.

I continued to be away for five days a week to the refinery. One day, Leo told me that he was leaving the Foundation as the refinery had hired him to be part of its staff. I was asked to give leadership to all the Fudeco projects. Since the refinery projects had urgency, I dedicated more time to them than for other projects. There came a point when Leo recommended that I too join the refinery as an employee. I pointed out that I should stay with Fudeco until the task analysis phase was completed, the bills were settled, and an interim report prepared. Accordingly, I stayed on with the project for four more months. I went through all the interviews that were necessary for me to be hired by the refinery. When I finished the interim report, the decision hadn't been taken yet for my employment. But, in a month's time, I was formally declared as an employee of VPC. I was hired as a Training Advisor. My initial assignment was to carry on with the project up to the final phase.

I requested a month to join the refinery so that I could take a short vacation to visit India before I started work; I wouldn't have been able to take time off for one year once I started working, and I hadn't visited India in over three years. The permission was granted. I resigned from Fudeco, took the cars to Devan's house (who had moved to the town next to ours), packed the suitcases, and left for India. Travelling to the other side of the earth with three small children is no joke. It is a journey that I will never forget in my whole life. In the first leg of our journey, we lost Rajeev in the Caracas airport at the luggage belt area. Since the airport was small, we located him quickly. The few seconds that we lost him were the most excruciating. I had to make sure that I and Melody did not run at the same time in different directions, leaving the baby and the four year old unattended. Fortunately, Rajeev was detained by the National Guard at the exit gate.

PANAM took us to the New York area where there was a storm. The plane flew above the storm and reached JFK airport but had to do some nose diving for the touchdown. All three children started screaming as their ears ached. Both the two older ones threw up. It was a mess, but the cabin crew was very understanding. We were picked up by Melody's uncle from Philadelphia. After spending two days with him and doing some shopping, we were on our way to the Philadelphia airport for the flight to JFK, and from there, to Bombay. But we arrived late to the Philadelphia airport and were checked in on the condition that we ran to the gate and reached it before it closed. We ran, but when I looked back, I did not see Rajeev. This was the second time he got lost in this journey. I went back, running with the carry-on, the super-eight movie camera, and the toys, only to locate him admiring the planes from the glass windows from a side gate. When we finally arrived at the gate, the door closed before our faces. We were told that the luggage had gone with the flight. We were put in another flight an hour later with another airline, and arrived at JFK with just half an hour to check in for the flight to Bombay. But the luggage had to be picked up from another terminal. I left Melody and the children at the terminal and ran to look for the luggage. When I returned, I had just fifteen minutes left to check in, clear the security procedures, and reach the gate. The people at the counter were very kind and called someone to detain the plane until we reached. We ran through all the security procedures and reached the gate to be greeted by the PANAM crew as the last passengers to board. All the passengers were looking at us with sympathetic eyes. I was drenched in sweat and felt very exhausted. But I consoled myself that we hadn't lost the flight. Losing the flight meant losing the flight to Cochin, which in turn meant spending any number of days at the Bombay airport.

We arrived in Bombay, on time, at mid-night. Rajeev refused to get up and walk to the exit. He just lay down on the aisle, saying that he was too tired. If I carried him, I wouldn't be able to carry all the hand carry items I had brought into the plane. We let everybody go ahead of us. We were at a loss as to how to handle the situation, when the captain himself came to our rescue. He carried Rajeev down the stairs. The first document to be checked was the health certificates. While I handed over the health certificates for revision, Rajeev sat down and peed. I was shocked and at a loss as to what to do. I asked around for some paper towels, when the officer himself handed over to me a piece of cloth. The officer explained to me that many children who arrive from foreign countries use the same spot to release themselves. I admired his sense of preparedness, understanding, and humor. We passed through the customs without problems. I got two porters to carry the luggage (there were no carts in those days in the airport); I carried Rajeev, Melody carried Ranya, and Roshni walked behind me. I had to walk fast to keep up with the porters who were in a hurry to finish the job and attend to other clients. There were a lot of people on both sides waiting for their loved ones to show up. When I looked behind, I saw Roshni being carried by a beggar with a beard and following me. I did not know what to do, to go back and get the child from him or to follow the porters who could walk away with the luggage. I preferred to follow the porters looking very often behind. I sent the porters away with generous tips. The beggar wanted an exorbitant amount for carrying the child. I argued with the beggar that he was not asked to carry the child. Then he resorted to blackmailing me by saying that he could have walked away with the child. I let him have the money as the taxi in line had been loaded, and the driver was impatient. We reached the airport hotel; the porter carried the luggage to the room, and we collapsed on to the bed. Suddenly, Melody remembered to look for the gold packet and found out that the suitcase in which it was packed was missing. I rushed to the airport to look for the taxi that brought us to the hotel. I located the taxi waiting in the line and recuperated the suitcase, which was in the trunk. The same taxi took me back to the hotel. I was happy to know that there was a system in place in the midst of what seemed chaos in the airport. The moment I appeared to make my claim, the dispatcher of the taxis attended to me immediately, located the taxi driver, scolded him for not taking out the suitcase from the trunk, and asked him to take it back to the hotel at no charge. The whole thing was dismissed as forgetfulness on the part of the taxi driver in the midst of so much hurry and confusion. I paid him something more, for he had lost his turn to load and had to queue once again. I took some rest, but soon had to return to the airport to reconfirm the reservation to Cochin. I had to fight with other passengers to be accommodated. Nobody respected queues. The airline attended to passengers who were accompanied by people who wielded influence. My name was not in the list of reservations, and I showed the ticket with an "OK". The officer told me to come back to the airport two hours before the flight and said the problem could be fixed. I went back to the hotel but knew that the problem would not be fixed that easily. There is an old saying in Venezuela, which when translated goes like this: "the devil is a devil more because of experience than for being a devil". My previous experiences at the Bombay airport warned me of trouble. I could not sleep. I could not think of sending away Melody and children and stay behind. We were at the airport without fail two hours before the flight. The officer who attended to me was nowhere to be seen. There was another officer in his place and pandemonium in front of him. Many people were complaining that they had lost flights. After waiting for one hour, I broke off the line and demanded that I be confirmed for the flight; the officer told me that the flight was full. I told him that the other officer assured me that the problem could be fixed. He asked me to wait around for the other officer to show up. Meanwhile, the passengers to Cochin were checking in. I was very worried that we would miss the flight. Fortunately, the other officer showed up, and I approached him for my case. He asked me to wait around. I knew that they wanted money, and I was prepared not to give in. I was prepared to raise hell. I saw several other passengers offering bribes. The security check-up call came for our flight, and we hadn't even checked in. I raised my voice and warned the officer that if the flight left without us, the airline would be completely responsible for all the damages that could result and the cost of accommodating five people in the hotel. At this moment, the head of the section walked in, enquired what my complaint was, and signed my ticket and asked me to check in for the flight. I let out a sigh of relief and rushed through the procedures to get into the plane. The flight was half empty. I cursed Indian Airlines that put me through so many problems with so many empty seats. During the flight, I schemed on how to punish the airline. I even visualized becoming the Prime Minister of India and closing the airline company that had become a monopoly with no sense of service. When the plane touched down after an hour and a half, I too touched down to the reality that my loved ones were waiting at the airport to receive us. I looked through the window but could not locate anyone. As soon as we deplaned, Melody's father broke through the barricade and came and picked up Rajeev and carried him off. He apparently knew someone in the airport. My father too came and carried off Roshni. The celebration began, and we forgot all that had happened to us in the journey.

Twenty six days after I landed in India, I was back on the plane, this time, alone, en route to New York, Caracas and Barquisimeto. I was nostalgic that I had left behind Melody and the children. I picked up one of the cars from Devan's house, got up at 3 AM, and drove five hours to report for work at 8 AM in the refinery on the appointed day. Leo was my supervisor, and he scolded me for having driven during such odd hours on lonely roads after such a tiring journey, and sent me to a hotel to sleep and return for work the next day. I will never forget the sweet and deep sleep I had.

CHAPTER TEN

Cooking Black Gold

That first step at 8 AM the next day was the beginning of a long journey in the petroleum industry. Until 1976, several transnational companies, and some local companies owned and operated the industry. The government nationalized all of them and grouped them under a corporation called The Venezuelan Petroleum Company (VPC). However, each individual company kept its own identity and operations under a new name and status known as an affiliate. I was getting into one of the affiliate companies. All new employees were given an orientation program, starting from the first day, in which, the business of VPC and that of the affiliate company were explained. This program was very handy and relevant to me to learn more about the petroleum business and the company I was getting into. It helped me identify myself with and appreciate the company more thoroughly. The orientation program lasted a whole week and included talks about the company's business, safety procedures and core values. The program also included individual meetings with managers and supervisors to get to know each other and to establish one-o-one relationships. I established very good rapport with all the people I met. Leo added one more week to my orientation program for me to have a first-hand experience with the refinery processes. I was assigned to different plants at different shifts to get to know the process, procedures and people responsible for the operation of the plants. This was a valuable experience because I never had such a close contact with plant operations people or the processes they controlled. I did the three eight hour shifts in every plant. The night shift was really difficult because of sleep deprivation. I was surprised to find out that the night shift personnel ate another meal at around 2 AM although all of them came after dinner at home. They also ate breakfast after they finished their shift at 6 AM. Thus, they ended up eating four meals per day. However, they spent a lot of calories walking around the plants in the cold nights. We all drive into a petrol station, but we are not aware of the sleepless nights spent by the operators to produce it. A third week was added, again at the request of Leo, to visit the division where crude oil was produced, which was located in another part of Venezuela. I also visited the corporate head quarters in Caracas where all the major decisions were made. VPC explored, produced, refined and marketed petroleum through three affiliate companies. Each affiliate carried out all these functions. In fact, they were competitors. The refinery that I worked for processed about three hundred thousand barrels per day. The country has a total capacity for refining of 1.5 million barrels of crude oil per day and has some gas processing plants. VPC employed directly around forty thousand people, of which ten thousand worked in my company and two thousand people were employed in the refinery where I worked.

The Venezuelan oil business is one of the biggest in the world. Venezuela to-day has a known reserve of forty billion barrels of light crude oil compared to the two hundred and sixty two billion barrels that Saudi Arabia has. However, Venezuela has a known reserve of two hundred and thirty six billion barrels of extra heavy crude oil, which makes it a potential producer, comparable to Saudi Arabia. At the height of production, Venezuela produced five million barrels per day. At the present rate of production, Venezuela has oil for over two hundred and fifty years. Light crude oil is petroleum with light components like gasoline, gas oil and other valuable derivatives which can be easily extracted by refining. Heavy crude oil is petroleum left with heavy components (the lighter components have evaporated), which are difficult to extract, by refining and so the whole process is relatively expensive. The technology to refine heavy crude oil has been invented only recently. Since I had a background in chemistry, I could easily understand the process of refining. There are refineries with very few plants, and there are refineries, like the one I was working for, with a number of plants. The bigness of a refinery depends upon the types, quantities and the qualities of the crude oil that it processes and the derivatives it produces. If it is light and free from contaminants, very few plants are necessary to refine it and extract the few derivatives that it contains. If it is heavy and several derivatives need to be produced, several plants are necessary for the processing. Gasoline is the most important derivative in any refinery; it is treated with some additives to make it a more efficient fuel for automobiles. Afterward, it is then transported, stored and sold in retail gas stations. Why is gasoline sold at different prices at different gas stations? There are several considerations that go into pricing gasoline sold at gas stations: the price of the crude oil, the cost of refining, the cost of transportation, the cost of storage, taxation charged by the government and the margin of the retailer. All these were things I learned in the orientation program.

After the orientation program, I met with my big boss, the human resources manager. He had met me during the recruitment interview, so our conversation was fluid. After informing him of my impression of the orientation program, we talked in general about the job I was going to do. At the end of the interview, the manager gave me a piece of advice which has stayed with me even today. He told me, "Joe, we know that you are a PhD, which is very important. However, what is more important for you in this company is how you relate to people, how you work with them and become part of the team. If you understand this, the sky is the limit to your progress in this company". I would remind myself of this advice many times in my career. I thanked God that I got a job with VPC, which was considered the best company to work for in Venezuela at that time. The employees of VPC were to a certain extent a privileged class, envied by the rest of the country because their jobs paid well, had stability and were socially respected. My brothers used to call me the "Venezuelan Sheik". Several of them came to visit me.

The company assigned me a four bedroom house in a new housing development and charged nominal rent. I transferred all the household goods and furniture from the apartment in Barquisimeto to the new house. Melody arrived one month after I had started work, and we got the house fixed and running. Roshni and Rajeev were admitted into a pre-school known as "Mama Chaun" (the nick name of the Chinese lady who ran the school). Every time the school bus brought Rajeev back to the house, he had to be lifted up from the seat as he was usually fast asleep. Mama Chaun told us that Rajeev had attention problems in the class, but we did not worry about it as he was very young. I loved gardening. I planted fruit plants all around the house, and I got immense pleasure in watching them grow. I usually woke up early in the morning and took care of the plants. Every new leaf or shoot captured my attention. I also bought a puppy for the children. The puppy grew up fast and started playing with my garden, biting and pulling out the young plants. I got so tired of replanting them that I decided to get rid of the dog. One day, early in the morning, I got the dog into the car while the children were asleep and drove it to the house of the person from whom I had bought it. When I returned, the children knew what I had done and refused to talk to me for a while. However, they got over it soon.

I had been assigned to training all the personnel that were working for the operation and maintenance of plants—around five hundred employees. I was fully responsible for the training of these employees to assure that they possessed the knowledge, skills and attitude that were required to do their jobs. The project that I was involved in the refinery as a Fudeco employee was re-contracted with an ex-employee of the refinery. However, I had to supervise the project. I gave personal attention to every employee under my care. I determined the knowledge, skill and attitude gaps of each employee for each current job and any future jobs foreseen in his or her career plan. Then I proceeded to determine a training solution that leveled each employee's gap. The training solution was a course, on the job training (OJT) or on the job experience (OJE). The course was one that was already designed and available to be taught, or custom designed. The OJT is usually a one-on-one or small group tutoring by a person who has a given skill. The OJE is the assignment of an employee to work as assistant to an experienced employee so that the former will learn by observing the latter doing the job. All three methods were used in the refinery. The first preference of the employee was to be sent for course instruction, preferably outside the country. All the employees used to be very friendly to me because they thought that I had influence in nominating them for training outside Venezuela. Truthfully, my influence was limited as those decisions were made by the manager of the employee, although the manager always sought my advice.

There was a group of Indian engineers working in the refinery who were recent arrivals. Because of a previous good experience with one or two Indian engineers, the refinery had recruited more of them. They came with their family and children, and the refinery provided them with housing and school. These engineers were very hard working. They would put in as many hours of work as were needed according to the expectations of their Venezuelan bosses. They used all available resources to promote their well-being in the company. They used the custom of inviting people for dinner lavishly. We were their frequent dinner guests. We too fell into the rat race and reciprocated the invitations. However, we slowly found out that the group got divided into small clichés, based on commonalities, self interests, mother tongues or previous acquaintances. These clichés were not openly visible, but everybody knew they existed. We deliberately avoided belonging to any particular group, although there was no lack of invitations and insinuations. The weekends were full of activities like beach parties, card games, picnics and visits to parts of Venezuela. The card game Fifty Six, which is played in every nook and corner of Kerala, was introduced by me to the group, and soon it became the most popular card game among the expatriates. I was elected as the President of the Indian Association; I organized feasts, parties, games, picnics and outings.

The refinery had weekend vacation facilities in several parts of Venezuela, including Caracas. If a reservation was available, the employee could take off Friday afternoon; spend Saturday and Sunday at the facility and show up for work on Monday morning. On one occasion, two Indian families drove to Caracas to spend the weekend there. On Saturday morning, they drove through the streets of Caracas to get to know the city. While driving in a particular street, they were caught by a policeman for driving in the wrong direction on a one-way street. They argued with him, saying that they did not know the city and that they did not know Spanish properly. One of them invited the officer to talk it over a drink in the families' hotel apartment. He gladly accepted the offer, and soon they were celebrating the encounter of the two cultures over drinks. Very soon the drinks ran out, and the policeman guided them to the shop where they could buy more. In the evening, the ladies prepared nice curry dishes, and the policeman ate to his heart's content. Later, he drove the whole group around the streets under the beautiful night lights of Caracas. One can read volumes about the culture and friendliness of the people of Venezuela from the behavior of the policeman. One can also conclude how strict the rule of law in the country was!

Roshni's fifth birthday was around the corner, and we planned to celebrate it by inviting a few of her friends. On the day of the feast, we decorated the house according to the children's taste. We decided to hold games in the garden around the house for the children, but the lighting was not enough and I decided to put up more lighting using an extension. In the process I caught a live wire and got a strong electric shock, the full wattage (the thermoelectric plant was just two thousand feet away) pull kept me held to the wire. I had the presence of mind to use all the adrenaline in my body to pull my hand away from the live wire and save my life. It was not easy. Can anyone imagine the tragedy that would have been if I were to be electrocuted to death? What could have happened if Melody and the children came to save me? They too could have been electrocuted. There may have been more deaths if other children or their parents intervened. I immediately ran to unplug the live wire so nobody else would touch it. Even to-day, when I think about it, a cold sweat runs through my body. I thanked God for having spared my life and the lives of all present that day.

Although I entered the company with a PhD, the advantage of the degree was very relative. A PhD title is very much appreciated in an academic environment, not in an industrial one. In the industrial environment, a professional degree with one or more of the following will take you far: a Godfather, the capacity to serve the boss and good salesmanship. The Godfather comes in the form of a family member or a relative (an uncle for example) or even a friend who works or worked as a manager or supervisor. I saw a number of people reaching managerial positions because they had somebody to pull them up. However, once the Godfather figure was gone, the employee began decelerating. Then there is the employee who invites the manager for dinner, visits his or her house often, plays golf or tennis with him or her, and does or him a lot of favors including shopping and taking his or her children to School. The manager in turn rewards the servile attitude of the employee by promoting him or her. They are noticed and resented by the other employees. Their career stagnates when they are no longer in favor of the manager or when the manager is changed. Of course, he or she will play the same trick with the new manager and may or may not succeed. There is also the employee who tries to impress managers, supervisors and even other employees with a presentation for a project or gets involved in social activities to be noticed and talked about. Such an employee stands a good chance to be included in projects and eventually be promoted. This can continue as long as the employee can impress others. However, the majority of employees do quiet work and wait patiently for the turn for recognition. I belonged to this category.

The company that I worked for was affectionately called "Mamaven" by its employees, a reference to the motherly attitude. She was every bit a mother to her children: caring, loving, understanding, encouraging, empowering, disciplining and forgiving. The employees felt stability at work and felt they could count on the company for all their economic and social needs. For example, when my Father died in India, I could not have arrived in time for his burial, so I did not go. Later, the company, without my asking, made an arrangement for me to attend two courses, one after another, one in Holland and the other in India. The courses were useful, but greater was the desire of the company to help me to visit my bereaved family. However, Mamaven was not perfect either. The culture of the company was fast paced. A lot of projects got started, a lot of procedures written, a lot of courses taught and a lot of people recruited. The staff lived from presentation to presentation, from meetings to meetings and from reports to reports. There was an emphasis on quantity at the expense of quality. Because everything needed to be done yesterday, many things were pushed through without considering all aspects. When there was money, ambitious projects used to be approved; when money ran out, the same used to be scraped, resulting in wasted money. Some people worked for their own benefits more than for the team. As a result, members of the same team used to contradict each other in inter-company meetings, making Mamaven lose credibility. The neighboring affiliate company was seen as more disciplined; all the reports were analyzed by a team and presented by the manager. When he spoke, nobody else spoke. If he did not approve, the report was not presented in a meeting; the representative of the affiliate company made an excuse saying that the report would be presented in the next meeting. However, when it was finally presented, everybody was part of it. In contrast, the Mamaven report, used to be prepared by one or two persons, and everybody else seconded it but were not fully identified with it. Still, I loved Mamaven and would not have felt at ease working for any of the other VPC companies.

I entered the company when it was in the height of expansion. Several new plants were added to produce new products. I was assigned the task of training the personnel that designed, constructed and operated the new plants. Several engineers were assigned to off-shore companies for training to learn how to install and operate the systems that we purchased from them. It was hectic for everybody in the project. Any delay meant much cost overrun. If one didn't have a balanced approach to work, home, and personal needs, one could go off the track. Sadly, one incident consternated all of us. One of the important managers in the projects killed his girl-friend and then killed himself. I knew the girl, who was from the neighboring refinery and a good engineer. Knowing him only during a brief period, I am not surprised that it happened. His personality was imposing, ambitious, and demanding, and he wanted things to happen his way. His anger consumed prematurely two lives that had had a lot more to contribute to society. The girl died victim of his emotional instability, and her family could not come to terms for a long time with her premature departure.

Apart from the new plants, the Company planned to build a new refinery. I was assigned as the training coordinator of the project. Much work was in progress. However, suddenly the price of crude oil started dropping, and the project had to be scrapped. The employees who were assembled to manage this project were sent back to the organizations from where they came. I had been with the project for one year. Instead of returning to my parent HR organization, I got transferred to the corporate office in Caracas. I visited Caracas to find out the exact nature of my job. I was received by the training manager with curtsey and respect. The manager said my education and experience were very useful for his organization. I was received equally well by others who worked in the organization. I visited the school in Caracas run by the Maristas, the same congregation that ran the school where Roshni was studying. They promised that a transfer for Roshni could be considered, but schools for the other children needed to be looked elsewhere as they did not have kindergarten sections.

The day came for me to say farewell to the refinery. I went around the operations and maintenance departments where I had trained several people and found several well wishers. I went to the HR organization and bid goodbye to all my colleagues; they all wished me well in Caracas. The next day, the truck came to pack the family belongings and move them to storage in Caracas until we got a place to live. We bid goodbye to the neighbors and drove to Caracas, taking with us the memories of one and a half years. We stopped at the sand dunes and had one final look. We also passed a truck that was carrying goats to the butcher shop.

CHAPTER ELEVEN

In the Metropolis

We reached Caracas after eight hours of drive and were put up by the company in an apartment in a hotel with cooking facilities close to the office. The next day, the manager of Human Resources in Caracas received me with so much kindness that I instantly took him as my adopted father. The manager did not allow any of his employees to work after the office hours unless it was necessary. He would come around to make sure that everybody left the office at 5.00 PM. If overtime was needed, permission had to be obtained. He would argue that if anyone needed overtime, either he/she had too much work (which needed to be reconsidered) or was not using the time efficiently (which also needed to be analyzed). I was entitled to a loan for renting a house or apartment as my residence. The manager told me to buy an apartment rather than rent one since I could get a loan from the company free of interest and almost a lifetime to payback. I had a very good experience with the apartments I bought earlier. The Manager saw me in the corridor and asked me if I had found a place to buy. I said I was not able to see one yet as I was occupied in settling down at work. He cautioned me that I should not fall in love with the first apartment that I saw just like some men fall in love with the first woman that they meet. He also told me that before he approved the loan, I should discuss with him at least six apartments or houses that I have seen. He even recommended that I see more than six. Accordingly, I went around seeing apartments that were advertised. Finally, I presented the six apartments that I had selected. The manager asked me to prioritize them based on my liking. He asked me to negotiate their price starting from the first preference. I was lucky enough to close the deal on the first preference itself. However, in order to buy it, I had to sell at least one of the two apartments I had in Maracay and Barquisimeto because the money in my possession, together with the loan, was not enough to cover the total value of the apartment. In fact, I decided to sell both, and they were sold in record time. I got the stay in the hotel extended for one more month while I got the paper work underway. Finally, two months after we moved to Caracas, I signed all the papers and moved into the apartment, just twenty minutes drive from the office. We were very happy with the apartment since the building had a lot of green areas and a good size swimming pool. The children went to the pool the same day we moved in and made a number of friends from the building. Of course, it was not the same as living in a house like the one we had in the refinery. Still, like the majority of people who lived in Caracas, we were happy that we ended up in an apartment of our liking. Roshni's School was just a fifteen-minute drive from our residence. There were a number of kindergartens nearby for Rajeev and Ranya to attend. There were several churches in the area, but the priest in the church closest to the apartment sounded great on Sundays and was even seen on TV regularly. This church became our parish. Finally we settled down, and the routines took over our life.

I was assigned for training all the geologists, geophysicists and petroleum engineers who worked for the exploration and production of crude oil. I was also asked to keep a corporate bird view of the training of refinery and petroleum production personnel in the sites. These responsibilities meant that I directly manage all the nominations for courses with a transnational company since most of these courses were in the areas of exploration, production and refining. Since my background was not very much related to exploration and production of crude, I requested to be sent for training in these areas. I was sent for a basic course on exploration and production to Holland which gave me a solid grounding on how petroleum is formed, explored and produced. All my notions about petroleum formation had to be revised as a result of this course. Petroleum is formed as a result of sedimentation that happens in river beds and deltas during millions of years. The land erosions bring into the river beds a lot of sand along with rich organic matter like the remains of animals and plants. A lot of algae and unicellular animals are developed which feed on the organic matter, eventually decaying and depositing to the bottom of the river bed. This process continues for millions of years, and organic matter gets deposited between sand layers. At a certain depth, the sand gets compressed to form a rock with a fruit cake like structure, with water and organic material trapped into the interstices. As the rock reaches a certain depth, it is subjected to certain pressure and temperature and behaves like a pressure-cooker, in which the organic matter in the interstices gets converted into natural gas and petroleum. The gas and petroleum start separating from water as they are lighter and start moving upward. At certain places, the rock that contains petroleum gets bent or folded because of faults in the earth and the petroleum and gas get trapped as it cannot keep seeping up and so get accumulated. These faults occur at different heights, and so different concentrations of petroleum get accumulated, some mixture being light in one place and some mixture being hard at another place. If the upward movement is not stopped, the gas and petroleum reach the surface of the earth's crust. The gas gets lost into the air, and the petroleum gets degraded at the surface.

Geologists and geophysicists locate the accumulation of petroleum using their professional techniques, which are not yet very precise science. When they discover an accumulation of petroleum (which is always associated with gas and water), the petroleum engineers bore some wells into the rock that holds the hydrocarbon mixture. They study the samples from the well and determine the characteristics of the petroleum. If the exploratory well yields good quantity of petroleum (they may hit a dry hole too), the engineers continue to bore different wells at different places in order to study the extent of the accumulation and evaluate the reservoir. If the study discovers a reservoir with a good probability of yielding enough petroleum, which can be exploited efficiently with existing technologies and produced with economic margins, the field enters into the production phase. In this phase, wells are bored at different places, conditioned to produce at maximum yield, crude pumped out, treated to separate the gas and water, stored in tanks and sold in the international market or refined to produce gasoline and other derivates. Once a well starts declining production, the petroleum engineers use several techniques to enhance the production. The present day techniques can extract only around thirty percent of the crude in place; seventy percent remains in the ground.

VPC sold most of its crude in the international market on long term contracts. This made it less vulnerable to price fluctuations, and it got a fair price for its crude. However, the international buyer could resell the crude in the spot market, where the highest bidder wins the day. In a market where there is a shortage of crude, a ship full of crude in the middle of the ocean, can change hands several times before it reaches a refinery; and thus makes the gasoline and other derivates all the more expensive. It was a challenging job, to plan and carry-out training for employees in whom the company depended to explore and produce petroleum as economically as possible. There were very few technical courses of good quality offered in the Venezuelan training market. The company mostly depended on the courses offered by the transnational company mentioned before. The company also made use of courses offered in the US and Canada by petroleum companies, third party training companies, universities and even by individuals. I used to travel to the US and Europe to evaluate these courses. Occasionally, I brought courses to be taught in Venezuela so that a number of professionals could participate in them. There were times when I used to be living out of hotels in and outside Venezuela. Those were difficult times for Melody as she had to manage the house alone with the three children, all going to school. She had to take and bring them back from three different schools, supervise their homework, pay all the bills, maintain the house and attend to all the social commitments. I tried as much as I could be at home so that I could help her.

One day, when I was sitting in my office, somebody knocked on the door, and I opened it to find a person of Indian origin. He looked like a priest and introduced himself as Father Bernard, working in a nearby parish. He was short, bald, dark and in lay clothes. He told me that he was from Kerala and had worked for the Catholic Charities in Delhi before he migrated to Peru as the guest of the Bishop of Lima. There, he worked to convert the members of the terrorist group Known as Shining Path, which was very active during the seventies and eighties. His job was to try to convince them to leave their terrorist activities and integrate themselves into the society to achieve their just causes by democratic means. Fr. Bernard was successful in converting many of them to peaceful means, and several of them even followed him to a place in Venezuela, where he had worked with a local terrorist group that had sprung up. After he had contributed to the disintegration of the group in Venezuela, Fr. Bernard was requested by another Bishop near Caracas to help him rebuild a church that was destroyed twenty years earlier in an earth-quake. He was appointed parish priest and took up the job of reconstructing the church. He had to start everything from the scratch, including getting people back to Catholicism as many of them had drifted to Evangelism. He erected a tent which served as a meeting place for mass and other spiritual services. He lost no time to push forward the reconstruction of the church. He organized a parish committee to help him plan, design, collect funds and build the church. He had very little budget from the Bishop. He met with local industry and business people and sought their participation, which was generously made available to him. He met with government officials to present his case and got a lot of help as the majority of these officials belonged to the Catholic Church. He demolished the remains of the old church and in its place built a new church in record time. The church was inaugurated by the president of the country. Fr. Bernard was visiting my company to get a donation of used furniture from the Board of Directors when somebody told him about me. That is how he came to meet me. He invited me, and my family to visit his church, which was just six months old.

We took the children the next week end to visit the church and attend mass. The interior of the church was very beautiful and yet simple and functional. It had a parish office with rooms for meeting, a dining hall, a guest bedroom and Father's bed room. The villagers immediately spread the message that Fr. Bernard's sister, nephew, nieces and brother in-law had come to visit him. We were instant celebrities in the village. Father took our children in his jeep to buy ice cream, and they were greeted as his nephew and nieces. The parish ladies used to bring him food which he used to share with his guests. Two girls helped him out with the parish activities, especially to teach catechism and to orient youths in their studies. One girl was from Peru, and a convert from terrorist activities. These girls turned out to be excellent cooks, and we relished their food and enjoyed their company. Our children enjoyed going to Father Bernard's church, and he even took them to other villages to serve as altar boys and girls during mass. The trip always ended up with generous portions of ice cream. We were frequent visitors of the parish.

We were informed by Rajeev's class teacher that he had problems of attention in class. Often he seemed dreaming in class. He made careless mistakes or did not complete the assigned work in class or at home on time. He had a hard time in concentrating to organize and complete a project, and if he completed, it required much fixing. I devised a strategy to increase his attention in class. I designed a format in which the teacher had to evaluate his attention every day. The format was stapled inside the back of his class book. At the end of the class, he had to take the class book to the teacher who checked the scale of his attention that day and I would review it with him in the evening. His attention improved a lot and his grades too. I used to check with the teacher if she was happy with the scheme and his performance in class. The teacher was very happy with what I had devised and even suggested to other parents to follow my scheme. My experiment went on for more than three years until he graduated from primary school. After a while, I did not cross check with the teacher and assumed that she was the one checking the box. When Rajeev became an adult he informed me that, towards the end of the primary School, it was his girl friend that checked the box. Any human process that is left to itself, without periodic check up, will lose effectiveness and even deteriorate. This is the lesson that I learned. Today, Rajeev is a fine professional working for a major bank in the US. My timely intervention and persistent follow-up saved him. The girls did not have many problems for studies. Still, I followed up on them by checking their homework. I talked to my children about future educational goals and career plans. I asked them every year who they wanted to become or what they wanted to do when they grew up. The description changed every year. I still have all those descriptions in my files. I wrote my own description of what I wanted to accomplish in life and read it out to them. None of my children turned out to be what they thought they were going to be, but the exercise kept them focused on their studies. We need a purpose in life to be focused, and the earlier it is defined, the earlier the course is chartered. I reviewed the progress report with my children and congratulated them on academic excellence if they deserved it and talked to them about issues if there were any. I rewarded them for good grades with money, and the sum was placed in a small box for each child; the keys were given to them to let them feel ownership.

Christmas is a time of enjoyment for children all over the world. In Venezuela, children await the arrival of Santa Claus with great expectations. One year, Santa arrives by helicopter, another year by fire engine, another year he descends by parachute. I used to take my children to witness the arrival of Santa to parks, to plazas and commercial centers. One day, Santa arrived to our building by a fire truck. The parents were asked by the organizers to hand over a gift for each child to be distributed by Santa. We had plenty of space in our building for Santa to play with the children. He even danced with them with live music. Finally, he distributed the gifts. Santa was exhausted with so much of activities and disappeared for a moment. Ranya was still looking for him to continue playing with him. She and a group of children went down the basement to look for him and found him smoking a cigarette in a corner. She was amazed that he smoked too. She came running to inform me that she found Santa smoking cigarette. I quietly told her that, since Santa Claus lived in North Pole where it is very cold, he had to smoke to keep himself warm. She seemed to accept the explanation. However, before going to bed, she asked me if Santa Claus was for real or he is someone made up. Of course, I told her that he was for real. Before long, Roshni joined the conversation. She told me that she suspected that Papa and Mama placed all those presents under the Christmas tree on the 24th night and that she didn't believe in Santa anymore. Rajeev too joined the conversation. He did not care if Santa was real or invented; he wanted Santa to bring the presents every year.

Melody's parents came to visit us, and we were so happy to receive them. One of the TV stations was shooting a scene around the pool, and they noticed our family. They requested if they could shoot in our house and present our family in the TV. We gave them permission, and they showed up one morning to shoot the footage. Melody's parents were included in the footage that was aired one week later; her parents were very happy that they ended up being shown in the national TV. We took them out to see places in and around Caracas. I took a vacation to take them to visit a friend of ours from India who lived eight hours drive from Caracas. The day before the trip, however, Melody's parents suddenly decided go back because the youngest daughter was sick and alone at home in India. We were sad that they had to go away so suddenly. We expected them to stay with us for at least a month. I was feeling guilty that I did not take vacation earlier and take them to see more places. I wanted to show them as many places as possible within the three remaining days. I mentioned to my father-in-law that there was a planetarium which was very much frequented by people. I had not seen it myself. I took my father-in-law to see it (Melody's Mother was not interested in it), but when we reached the place, the planetarium was closed for maintenance as it was a Monday. I was sad that I could not show him that either. I decided to go to the office and ask them if they would allow us to enter the facility just to have an idea what a planetarium looked like. I invented a lie that my father-in-law was a professor of astronomy in India (he in fact was a professor of physics) and that he would be happy to see their installation and compare it to the planetarium that he was in charge of back in his country. The planetarium was run by military, a fact that I discovered only then. The Colonel, who attended me, told me that he would not only run us through the facility, but also would make a demonstration (like the one given to the public) just for the two of us. I was flattered, but was nervous at the proposal that my lie would be discovered; but the poker face in me came up and I decided to accept the Colonel's offer. I explained to my Father-in-law what was going on, and he decided to play the game too. My father-in-law rose up to the occasion when I introduced him as professor of astronomy from the University of Madras. The Colonel ran us through the installation and started the show with the night sky of Caracas and the change of positions of the stars and planets at different periods of time. He stopped for a break, but before continuing the presentation, he asked my father-in-law what type of equipment he had in his planetarium, to which he fumbled something in English. Since neither I nor the Colonel understood what he said, I consulted with him and came up with the answer that it was Japanese make. I could feel the sweat that was running down on his body and the heavy beat of my heart. The Colonel asked us the year the equipment was made to which we answered 1950. Fortunately, he did not ask more questions but observed that he particularly liked the German model more than the Japanese (the equipment he was using was German). He continued with the presentation, and we asked him to cut it short since the maintenance people were waiting outside to enter. We ran out of the planetarium after thanking the Colonel, both of us sweating. My stunt had worked, but we both could have ended up in the military jail too if we had been discovered.

One day, I approached the Indian Embassy in Caracas to get my passport renewed. There were some Mother Teresa Sisters sitting on the bench waiting to be attended. I noticed that one of them was Mother Teresa.

In fact, she was sitting by my side. I didn't recognize her initially, but once I did, struck a conversation with her. She was very gentile to enquire all about me and my family. I invited her to my house to meet the rest of the family, but she excused saying that they were not allowed to visit individual families except for their charity work. She requested me to help out her sisters who are close to Liz's house in Kerala, India. There are some Mother Teresa Sisters houses in Venezuela, and we used to visit two of them in and around Caracas. These houses are located in the poorest areas where security is very low. But the Sisters are well protected by the people who live around them. Even the anti socials protect and take care of them. We were regular visitors of one of these houses. We were amazed to see how the Sisters took care of the sick children, some of them even picked up from the streets. One of them was a deformed child thrown into the garbage and picked up by the Sisters. Every child suffered from some form of physical or mental disability. The Sisters would look after them as their own children. They were cleaned, bathed, dressed and fed by their own hands. These children could not even say "thank you" in any adequate manner, and the Sisters showed them the same unconditional love day in and day out for years. I had never fully understood the meaning of "unconditional love", but after seeing how the Mother Teresa Sisters took care of the children, I have understood its meaning. I have seen the children grow up, and some of them even attend school. Only if, one is convinced of the value of what one is doing, can the children be looked after the way Mother Teresa Sisters do.

When Ranya was ten years old, she surprised us one day while we were driving her back home after school that she knew all about how she was conceived and born. We asked her to explain to us what the teacher had told her in the class, and she recited without any blush the process by which a child is conceived and born. I gave hundred marks for her knowledge of the whole reproductive system. Ranya used to surprise us other times too. One day she asked me for some money with which to buy a birthday present for her friend Gabriela. I told her that she had enough money in her savings box to buy the present. However, she came out saying, "I earned that money; that is not for spending; Papa, you give me money to buy the birth day present". I retorted her, "So my money is for spending while yours is for saving! I am not going to give you money while you have your own". She had to spend her own money to buy the present, but she taught me a great lesson. We value the money that we earn; money earned by other people is to be spent, even if they are our parents'. What a great lesson Ranya taught me! I think that those parents who work hard day and night, sweat their blood, even amass wealth by illegal means to give to the children haven't learned this lesson. When we pass on to our children money that they really don't need, we are breaking the law of God who told Adam that he will have to earn his bread by the sweat of his own brow. When we give our children superfluous money, we are going against this commandment. In fact, we are even doing them harm. We are converting them into parasites, teaching them to live on other people's sweats, even if they are the parents'. They will eventually lose the capacity to win their own bread. I wonder if people think about these things when they try to earn money by hook and crook in order that their children have it. They will spend it away in the long run. There was a well-known minister in charge of industry in Venezuela who made a fortune and set up several companies and banks. There was a time when several important industries and banks in Venezuela belonged to his family. He had two boys, and they were there to enjoy papa's fortune. The father died of a heart attack, and in no time all the fortunes were squandered. All the companies were sold, and all the banks went bankrupt. To-day, this family does not hold any company worth mentioning.

I had always wanted to make some extra money by working on a hobby during weekends. I was interested in agriculture. I saw a piece of land in a mountainous area, outside Caracas. There was a cultivation of pineapple in the land. I thought it was good buy as the land would appreciate over time and I could do some cultivation meanwhile. I took Melody and Fr. Bernard to have a look at it. They thought it was unsuitable; it was practically ravine to their perception. I gave up the plan, but Fr. Bernard was on the lookout for a property for cultivation. One day, Fr. Bernard informed me that there were thirty acres of agricultural estate for sale. I went with Father and looked at it. Half of the estate had tangerines and orange trees with fruits. There was a house for the care-taker. I thought that it would be good for the children to play around and explore the nature. I also thought we could pay for the cost of labor to develop the estate by selling the existing fruit production. It was just two hours away by car from Caracas and ideal for one day outing. I even thought that I could cultivate black pepper in the empty land. We were cultivators of black pepper back at home in India. I talked to some of my friends, and one of them showed real interest in the project. We both went and saw the estate and decided to buy it. The boy who was already working in the estate showed interest in continuing and even offered to be the care taker. My friend talked to another friend, and he too joined the project. I went and paid the money and came back with the documents in hand. We were very enthusiastic about the estate and dreamt of harvesting a lot of black pepper, which was mostly imported then for local consumption. There were some experiments conducted by a university for black pepper but were not yet at the production stage. We cleaned the estate of all weeds for the children to run around. The children and ladies were excited about the estate during the first two visits. After that the ladies dropped out as they had other priorities. The children too dropped out after a month as all the hatched birds flew away. The first crop of oranges and tangerines was quite good. We decided to sell them on our own in the Caracas wholesale market and so we brought them on Saturdays and sold them on Sundays. We were making enough money to pay the workers and to buy implements, fertilizers, weed killers and pesticides. I approached the university nursery to get black pepper cuttings. I got some and brought them to the estate and planted them. Poles were installed for the creeper plant to hold on to and climb. However, we found out that the workers were not very productive. They were not completing the jobs they were assigned during the week. They worked every Saturday morning when our routine visit was scheduled. The rest of the week they did pretty little as there was nobody on the spot to supervise them. When we pointed out that the assigned work was not completed, they would put forward all kinds of excuses. We tried to recruit other people for work, but they were scarce in the locality. It came to a point when we realized that we were losing money instead of making a profit. We got one more friend to join the group to raise more capital. Very soon, we lost that too. We had no other choice than to sell the estate. We sold it at a loss but consoled ourselves that we enjoyed the experiment, learned something about agriculture, ate a lot of fruits, had a good lunch and drank enough beer on Saturdays. The most important lesson that we learned was that in agriculture, either you invest good money and run it as any other business, or you invest in a small plot to live in it and make your living out of it. We were weekend agriculturers trying to run the business on a shoe string and on the remote control, which invariably could not work. We spent ten thousand dollars each to learn that lesson—a costly lesson.

Fr. Bernard was attending one week retreat in the Bishop's house when he found some blood in his stool. He immediately rushed back to Caracas and went to see the doctor. All the necessary tests were performed, and some polyps were discovered in the large intestine that had become cancerous. He was operated to remove the polyps. He started chemo and continued with his daily work schedule and even doubled his parish activities. He was a man on the run to get things done in half the time. He built a health care center by the side of the church. He built a vocational school with several specializations for the children of the parish. He started building an orphanage. He had touched some interests of the local business community, especially the owner of a clandestine bar located at the back yard of the orphanage. Father had many generous donors who encouraged him to go forward with his projects. He was very dear to many of the Indian community members. He went for another check up and the cancer had spread to his liver. He tripled his efforts to complete his projects; he knew he was short of time and he did not have a successor who would be equally passionate about them. Now he was like a heated up engine running at two hundred miles speed. He could have collapsed any time. I took him to some alternative medical treatments, but he was deteriorating every day. I could see that he was prepared, resigned to the will of God but kept on his feet even though they were slowly giving way.

I got a call from home that Melody's father had a heart attack and had passed away. Again, we were in tears. We were reminded of all the good time we had with him four years ago when Melody's parents visited us. Melody took the next flight to be at home for his burial. She spent one month with her mother and family members and returned to Venezuela. We continued our existence with a heavy heart knowing that Fr. Bernard could be the next one to go.

I was offered a job in a refinery operated by VPC in Curacao, one of the Caribbean Islands, and I went with Melody and children to check out the job, the school facilities and the island before I accepted the offer. We were received by former colleagues who also had been assigned to the island refinery. I was interviewed by the Human Resources Manager who was well known to me, the same one who was the HR Manager in the previous refinery. I accepted the job and visited the school where the children were to study. We were shown around the school, and we liked it. We were shown some houses to choose from for us to live. We were excited about the possibility of living again in a house and sending the children to an English medium school. The school our children were attending in Venezuela was Spanish medium. English medium schools in Caracas were very expensive, and we could not afford them. I was asked to start working in the island refinery as soon as possible. It was going to be just an internal transfer, but with a limited time period. I did not have enough time to wind up in Caracas and move the family to the island and, so I decided go alone for a month. Besides, the children's School was to close for annual vacations only after a month. We put the children through a crash course in English, paid by the company. They loved the course and picked up the American accent. We put the apartment for sale through an agent and I reported for work in the island as promised. There was a charter flight operated by VPC for the employees of affiliates to travel back and forth the island. I used to take the flight on Monday morning and return on Friday evening. The apartment got sold very fast. The day came for the final move, and a big truck showed up at our apartment building to pack our belongings. We shipped only ten cubic feet to the island. The rest was stored in Caracas. After sending off our belongings, we checked into a hotel at company expense. The children went straight to the refrigerator in the room for chocolates. They were disappointed when they found out that I had to pay for them, but they already had their first fill. The next day we took the charter flight to the island and bid goodbye to the Venezuelan shores.

We came back after one week to see Fr. Bernard as he was hospitalized. He was still full of cheer. We spent the weekend with him in the hospital, but we knew the end was near. We thought we could return and see him after a week. He wished us well and blessed us. We were in tears when we left him. We were waiting to board the plane at the terminal when one of our friends called and informed that Fr. Bernard was dying. By the time we reached his bedside, he was gone. He was buried the next day, and we took pictures and videos which were sent to his family in India. We haven't come across another person who resembled Jesus Christ more than Fr. Bernard. We returned to the island and settled down to the new job, house, school and surroundings.

CHAPTER TWELVE

The Bon Bini Island

The first time we arrived in the island refinery, two petroleum tanks were on fire. I could see from the plane those tanks, emitting large columns of smoke and the fire engines pouring water on the neighboring tanks to keep them cool. The common practice is to let the fuel burn off in the tanks because there is no efficient method to extinguish such a large fire. Since the nearby tanks with crude or more flammable products can catch fire easily by convection, they are cooled down by pouring water on them, thereby decreasing such a possibility. When we reached the terminal, there was nobody from the refinery to receive us; we had to find our way to the hotel where we had our reservations. I was not superstitious, but the fire and the failure of the refinery personnel to show up left me with a foreboding of more troubles to come. This time, when we were coming to settle down in the island, some of our Indian friends who had worked with us in Venezuela (who were there also as assignees) came to receive us at the airport.

They accompanied us to the hotel and then to dinner in our honor, held in one of their houses. We felt at home with so many known faces. The word "Bon Bini" means "welcome" in Papiamento spoken in the island. The welcome helped disappear half of our fears of coming to an unfamiliar place. There were other families too that were recent arrivals from India. They were recruited in India as expatriates and brought to the island to work in the refinery. The HR Manager was repeating the same successful experiment he had employed in his previous job in a Venezuelan refinery. We met almost all of them in the welcome party and were pleasantly surprised to know there were other expatriates too in the island who belonged to the Indian business community that had established in the island since a long time.

We took the children to the American School, and they were admitted into the grades to which they were promoted in Venezuela. The children were very happy with the first impression of the school. They had a good opinion of all their teachers. They found out that they could defend themselves quite well in English. I bought two cars, one for Melody to take the children to school and to do house errands and the other for me to drive to work. We were assigned a big old house in the housing complex where all the Venezuelan expatriates lived. The house was built by the transnational company that previously managed the refinery for its expatriates and local managers. The compound was big compared to that of some newer houses. There was enough space for a beautiful garden, but who could pay for the cost of water which was processed from sea water? Still, we cultivated some plants that grew well in spite of the salty winds. Bougainvillea grew so well in the island that we concentrated on them, and we had some of the best specimens in the island. Everyone who passed in front of our house looked at them and admired them.

I was to report to Andres Porras whom I had known in the Venezuelan refinery and of whom I did not have a good impression. I knew I had to report to him before accepting the job, and I was not very happy about it; still, I accepted it because of the possibility of an English medium education for my children and the chance to earn a salary in more hard currency. During the orientation program, I had the chance to meet with all the managers of the refinery to know what they were responsible for and to establish a personal and working relationship with them. I felt from the very start that there was something strange about the place; there were many issues and even conflicts below the apparent calm atmosphere. The local employees talked only about what was necessary and were cautious about what they said. For me, freedom of expression and absence of fear are the acid tests of contented people. I felt that the employees in the island refinery did not feel they had all the freedom to say whatever they wanted to, and, so they said very little and looked left and right to who was listening. I felt there were several conflicts at different temperatures in several pressure cookers.

Initially, my responsibility was to look after the scholarship program, sponsored by the refinery for the high school graduates of the island. They were to study in Venezuelan universities under a mutual agreement that after graduation the student would work for the refinery. The process involved the promotion of the program in the local high schools, selection of candidates, improving their Spanish, getting them admitted to the universities, travel and housing of students, monthly payments, academic and administrative controls, graduation and employment. When I took over the program, there were six students already in the universities in Venezuela, and ten were getting prepared for admission.

I tried to make friends with the neighbors with whom I shared a common fence. One of them was my friend from Venezuela, and the other a total stranger. I looked for him when he came out of the house and tried to strike a conversation. He was living alone and turned out be a wonderful person. He introduced himself as TJ of Belgian descent, born and brought up in South Africa. He invited me for drinks and told of his exploits as a pilot in South African army; and the sorties of bombings in which he participated in the African wars during the sixties. After his resignation from the army, he worked for a private company as a pilot on dares devil missions; and transported persons in war zones. He rescued some people affected by the bloody coup in 1972 in Chile. TJ was working as a pilot for the Antillean Airlines. After drinking till late night, he would get up early in the morning and report for duty. He used to fly the route to Miami.

We were devotees of the Blessed Virgin Mary, and she is very much worshiped in Venezuela. Of all the Blessed Virgins in Venezuela, the most well known is "Virgin de Coromoto". The story goes that the Blessed Virgin appeared to an indigenous boy in the year 1452 several times and asked a shrine to be built in a place known as Coromoto. The shrine was built since many centuries, and many people go there to pray to her.

The night before we left for the island, Melody dreamt that she was in a new church where there was a statue of Virgin de Coromoto and that the Blessed Mother stretched her hand and touched her face and blessed her. She told me of her dream and did not know what to make of it. The next Sunday after we reached the island, we asked around for a Catholic church to attend mass. We were told of a church nearby, and the first thing Melody noticed was the statue of the Virgin de Coromoto. The Church was even named after her. We never expected to come across a church dedicated to her in the island, and then we understood the significance of the dream. It became our parish church.

The island was a former Dutch colony and presently a Dutch Protectorate. When I was there, the island population was about two hundred thousand, of which ninety percent were African in origin, and the rest were Dutch white settlers and immigrants from Latin American countries. Several centuries ago, it used to be a hub for slaves, brought from African Countries. The major economic activities were the refinery, a dry dock (ship repairing yard), a free port and tourism. The refinery was the biggest source of employment, with direct jobs for about two thousand people and indirect jobs for about five thousand. The island was very arid, and so there was practically no agriculture. All that grew in the island was cactus, and goats were found everywhere. The food was practically imported—meat from Colombia, dairy products from Holland and grains, vegetables and fruits from Venezuela. Manufactured goods entered from all over the world through the free port and were exported to the nearby countries. Water was as expensive as gasoline. Every time we flushed the toilet, we felt a few dollars had gone down the drain. There was one Cinema Theater, two ice cream parlors, two supermarkets, a few restaurants and several shops, mostly belonging to Sindhis of Indian origin, selling clothes, electronic goods and other manufactured items.

The refinery was more than seventy years old, built by transnational company from Holland. This company was producing crude in Venezuela, and most of the crude refined came from there. In the 1980s, the refinery was no more economical to operate, and, the company decided to close it. Thousands of people were to lose their jobs. Thus, the local government bought the refinery and decided to operate it with another company. The island government approached VPC and offered good terms for it to operate under a lease contract. VPC accepted the offer as the refinery was originally built to refine the crude it produced. All the supply processes were in place. All that VPC needed to do was to bring its crude, refine it and sell the products. There was an excellent deep water bay where big tankers could approach the refinery to bring crude and to transport products. It was a perfect symbiosis between VPC and the island refinery. VPC brought its own management team and other support professionals. I belonged to this contingent of expats. However, the local refinery personnel never liked the Venezuelans in general and the VPC management in particular. The island people, for many years, have disliked the Venezuelans coming to the island and showing off their petrodollars. They never wanted the Venezuelans to manage their refinery. They had no choice other than to accept them because there was nobody else interested in operating it. The management had adopted an assertive style, which the employees, resented. They were accustomed to the management style of the previous company, which they said was friendlier. The VPC management knew they were not welcome and were seen as a necessary evil by the employees, and so they adopted an authoritarian rule. The orders were passed down from above, and the employees carried them out. Everyone felt like the poke of the grinding wheel at the service of the management. The meetings were to inform what needed to be done. Opinions were solicited, but the management took the final decision; and was often-times seen as arbitrary by the employees. The human resources group came up with some actions and plans during the total quality sessions, only to be told by the manger that those things were not necessary to be carried out. The managers assumed that the employees would not be well disposed towards the new "owners," and so they had to be told what and how to do things. This approach tacitly led them to use coercion, implicit threats, and tight controls and close supervision. If one looked beyond the surface, one could see the long faces the employees carried around inside them. The hard approach resulted in low-output, hostility and hard-line union demands. The labor contract discussion lasted for six months and resulted sometimes in strikes for the final approval. During the strike, the staff operated the refinery. I had to work twenty-four-hours shifts to keep the refinery running.

The managers set themselves as a separate class. They even had a separate wing where all the managers had their offices. One had to use one's pass to have access to their area. The management wing was called the "fish tank" because the access to the area was through a large glass door. All could see the managers moving around inside like fish in the tank. Although I could understand why the managers resorted to the tactics they were using, I could not identify with them. I believe in winning people by frank and open discussion and making them feel that they are part of the deal. I believe that people will rise to any occasion and will go the extra mile provided they are convinced that the company valued them as employees, trusted in their capacity and sincerity, empowered them to carry out their responsibilities, showed interest in their career development and gave a salary with which they could have a decent living. When people feel satisfied with the work environment, they will do their work to the best of their ability. If the work is a source of frustration, the workers will play the game just to stay in the court. I personally did not feel good at all with the new work environment. I was very happy with the work environment in Caracas, but the island refinery was totally a different world. Most of the managers were known to me, and some of them were my friends. I could not understand how they could accept being part of a group that was considered snobbish. There were rumors that some of them were even corrupt, taking commissions for work contracts. In my own presence, one manager was complaining to another manager that he was being unjustly accused of being corrupt. My boss, Mr. Porras, was totally identified with the management philosophy. We were mentally far apart from each other. Since I did not belong to the management group, and given my personality and education for fairness to the employees, I was a misfit from the beginning. I was expected to work any number of hours beyond the closing time. I was not used to this. I was welcomed with suspicion by the local people because I was a representative of VPC. I was not seen as a good representative of VPC by the management. Mr. Porras took my lack of total support to the management as treason. I could feel the coldness of some managers towards me. One of my friends, seeing me going into a no-man's land, tried to help me out, but it didn't work either. My only chance of survival was to be part of the VPC team; and playing by its own rules, which was not acceptable to me. I could not walk away from the job because I had signed a contract for two years. I could have asked for a release from the contract and returned to Caracas, but I wanted the children to continue in the American School. I needed the money, too. Hence, I decided to continue against all odds. I could not swallow it, for it was bitter, nor could I spit it out, for it was sweet enough. It was a delicate rope walk with every chance for a hard fall.

The island is a tourist spot. Its beaches are gorgeous with crystal clear water and white sands. Most of them seemed artificial because they were located between steep cliffs; and that made the beaches all the more attractive. As one drove along the coastline, one came across roads leading to beaches. The beaches were full of local people and tourists during the weekends. Some of the tourists were topless at the beach, a scene I was seeing for the first time. The children, at first, did not know what to do about it—to look or not to look—but soon they got used to it. There were a lot of coral growth and colored fish, so snorkeling was a favorite sport. One would visit more than one beach during the day. One day, I saw a busload of tourists come to a beach, change dress and jump into the water and leave the beach after an hour to the next one. We coincided with the tourists at several beaches. The island had a floating bridge, which opened for ships to get into the bay to unload their cargo or to let the tourists on land. People stood at the shore and watched how the bridge opened up, and the ships go by; they could practically touch them. It was an awesome feeling to see such huge ships so near. The island was one of the stops for cruise ships, and it was a special sight to see the tourists go by.

Another attraction of the island was the casinos. Practically every hotel had a casino. On weekends, especially on paid Friday nights, the local men (and some women too) visited the casinos to try their luck. They drank and played; invariably, many of them left early morning broke. However, the local men would stop on the way to pick up some vegetables and meat from the market for the day's soup. Many tourists also came from the neighboring countries to the casinos. In the two years I was there, I visited the casinos twice. After losing my twenty dollars, I sat at the bar to observe the people. Once, a young man was sitting by my side. We entered into a conversation, and I found out that he was from Maracaibo, the second largest city in Venezuela. I asked him how much he had lost, and he told me of an exorbitant amount. I was startled by the candor of the young man and the amount of money he had lost. I asked him how often he came to the casinos, and he replied that he came every month. I was curious to know where he got so much money to lose, and he told me that the money belonged to his father. He also added that his father made it illegally, and he was helping his father to get rid of it. If the children suspect that the money is not honestly earned, they will get rid of it more quickly. Ill-gotten money is earned at the expense of somebody's lunch. God will find the means of returning that money to the society through their own children. Here is a real story to illustrate the point. There was an Italian family who owned a hotel in Venezuela. I used to stay there once in a while. The family had made plenty of money, some of it by buying and selling stolen goods, especially gold, according to local gossip. They had a son who got mixed up with a local girl, got her pregnant, and he was forced to marry her. She soon took control of the hotel and kicked the in-laws out. The man who made all the money was soon in the grave from a massive heart attack. His wife ended up returning to Italy. The money earned illegally from the local residents was returned to them through the hands of a local girl.

I had taken the second group of scholarship students to the Venezuelan universities. I had to spend one week in settling them down. One morning when I got up, the television stations were announcing that there was a coup taking place in Venezuela. All the troop movements were shown on television. Many people were dead, but the coup had been put down. The leader was caught in his hideout. He declared that he was calling off the coup for the time being and surrendered to the authorities. Melody and the children were very much worried that I was in Venezuela in the midst of the melee. I was also a little worried that my return flight would get delayed. The next day, life started returning to normality. I returned to the island as planned. Eight months later, a military coup took place in Venezuela again; and this time I was in the island. The coup was again a failure and the leaders either escaped or were jailed. Two coups in one year made the leaders reflect on the state of the country. The president was impeached for corruption and was jailed. He was replaced by a well known scholar until elections were held. The candidate who was an ex-president won the election. The country settled down into a tense calmness. Old discontents simmered below the surface.

We decided to take a vacation to Orlando and visit Disney World and other attractions. I told my neighbor pilot TJ about our trip, and he invited us for a drink the previous night. We were afraid that TJ would fly our plane after all those drinks. We asked him if he was flying our plane to Miami, and he said he was probably going to another city. After one more drink, we left and got ready for the early morning flight. We saw TJ going early in the morning to the airport. One hour after we took off, TJ appeared and welcomed us aboard. He even sat by my side for a while, and when I asked him who was flying the plane, he said he had put it on automatic pilot. He ordered us some drinks and left for the cockpit. I was wondering if TJ was sober enough to land us safely in Miami. The plane landed in what looked like a different city. It was a perfect landing though. Upon inquiring, I found out that the plane had landed in Haiti. The touchdown in Miami too was perfect. TJ was a pilot of exceptional caliber. We took a rental car and drove to Orlando. The hotel was very comfortable, and the children enjoyed the lunch buffet in the restaurants. We loved Disney World, Epcot Center and the Dolphin show. In Disney World, Rajeev was very impressed with the Caribbean Forest tour, where the tourists were taken on a boat through jungles with crocodiles which looked real; and were jumping at them in every nook and corner. At the end of the trip, he told me that after his graduation from the university, he would love to work in Disney World as a tour guide. When I told Rajeev that the tour guide was probably bored to death for having to give the same speech day in and day out, he told me that he would work there as manager and not as a tour guide. I told him that he would have to study very hard and obtain a degree from a prestigious university with good grades to get a job as manager in Disney World. He thought for a while and said that he would rather be a veterinarian as planned in the New Year resolution. After a week, we drove back to Miami, returned the car and flew to New York to visit three of my younger brothers who lived there. The family get-together was a good opportunity for the cousins to meet and get to know each other. We returned to the island via Miami after one week of enjoyment in New York.

The carnival celebrations in the island are said to be the third in grandeur after Brazil and Trinidad. It was a spectacle that stayed in our mind for many years. Several months were taken up in preparation for the event. Each important company, institution or organization in the island sponsored and/or participated in the carnival parade every year. The group consisted of any number of people, even up to hundreds. Every year, each group, selected a theme to be presented and prepared the costume that described it. The carnival celebrations lasted three days; the parades took place during two days. The first parade was a trial, and the second was real. The public lined up to watch the parade, which took more than three hours. Galleries were built on both sides of the street along the route for the convenience of spectators. It was a thrill to watch some presidents of companies, institutions and organizations put on the costume and march along with their employees. The colors and designs were so attractive; the music was specially selected for the occasion; the allegoric carousals were well designed and decorated. The refinery had always a theme related to petroleum. The Christmas and New Year celebrations in the island were equally enjoyable. Many houses were decorated with lights of all colors. We used to go around at night to see the lighted houses. Some houses were open to the public. On the 24th and 31st nights, we climbed the highest mountain near the capital to watch the fireworks taking place in all directions. It lasted an hour and was very comparable to that of Caracas. People spent all their savings on these celebrations and, in January, pinched the pennies. The joy of Christmas and New Year was worth the few days of crunch stomach in January.

I was getting hints that I would return to Caracas after the two years of assignment, and it was going to create a serious problem. Roshni was completing her eleventh grade in the island, and she needed to complete the twelfth grade to qualify for the American High School Certificate. In Venezuela, the high school is completed at the eleventh grade. If she returned to Venezuela, she would have been in the limbo, without a high school certificate. Without the certificate, she could not have applied for admission to the university. Studying the twelfth grade at the American School in Caracas was no option as we could not afford it. We could have requested a high school certificate equivalency from the Venezuelan Ministry of Education, but that would have taken years to process. The logical thing was for me to stay on in the island for one more year for Roshni to complete the high school. I asked Mr. Porras if there was any plan for my return to Caracas, and he told me that it was true that I would return at the end of the school year. I made him aware of the educational problem for my daughter, but he told me that the company could not take care of individual problems deriving from transfers. I told him that I wanted to refer the case to the Human Resources Manager, but he said that the HR Manager was retiring and that a new HR Manager was taking over. I decided to wait for the new HR manager to arrive and settle down to raise the issue with him. The HR manager in office retired and settled down in the island itself. I was invited for the send off party, and I thanked the manager for his consideration and care towards me since the first day we met in the refinery in Venezuela, thirteen years earlier. His successor also was present, and I was introduced to him. I did not know him, but he seemed a good person. I had heard only good things about him. The new HR manager settled down without delay and asked to meet with me to have first hand information on the scholarship program. We had a pleasant conversation over lunch, and the manager asked several questions. I raised the educational issue of my daughter and requested an extension of my contract for one more year. He promised that he would study the problem and come back with a decision. He suggested that we get together again for lunch to share notes.

I quietly started preparing myself mentally to return to Caracas, but I had no idea as to how to resolve the problem of my daughter. I alerted Melody that there was the possibility that we would return to Caracas. In one of the trips to Caracas, I went to the previous school of children and enquired the possibility of their readmission. The principal told me that he could not guarantee anything, but asked me to return to school with the family once we were in Caracas. There was no solution in sight for Roshni's problem. I was becoming a pressure cooker inside on slow fire. The doctor prescribed me a small dose of pressure pill. He also asked me to take some sort of exercise, and so I started jogging. The jogging session ended up into a running session. I finally ended up running five kilometers every day. I got so confident at running that I registered myself for a 10 km marathon. I got a physical check up before the marathon and got certified to run. On the day of the marathon, I started running well, but as I was reaching near the 5 km mark, my feet started giving way. I finished the first 5 km running and continued the other 5 km walking and finished the race gasping. The lesson that I learned was that if one wants to run a marathon of 10 km, one has to practice running 10 km, nothing less than that. I also took to fasting as a result of reading a book on the subject. I was so convinced about the benefits of fasting that I began practicing it once a week. At the end of the day, I felt even stronger than other days. I ran the 5 km on the fasting day, and I was even less tired. I extended the fast to two days and felt excellent. I wanted to continue for five days when my family complained that I was taking it too seriously without knowing its long term effects and without consulting a doctor. However, I continued the one day fast per week.

When I was doing my physical for the marathon, there was an employee doing his medical checkup. He was working in HR but in a different department. We talked for a while in the waiting room. This employee was leaving for vacations after the physical checkup which was required for the vacation bonus. He was medically declared fit by the doctor. That evening he took off from the local airport to Amsterdam and half an hour into the flight, he got a heart attack and died in the plane. His wife and two children were shocked, and so were the passengers. The plane could not return and land in the airport because the runway was short for the weight it was carrying. The plane continued the flight to Amsterdam. The body came back in the return flight, and the burial took place the next day. All who attended the burial came away wondering what kind of physical check up the person had received and ended up dying the very same day.

I was called to the office of the HR manager on a Friday afternoon and was informed that my contract was extended for one more year in view of my daughter's need. I was very happy and told everyone the good news. Some of our Venezuelan friends showed some surprise at hearing the news; I concluded that they were expecting me to return to Caracas. I even told Mr. Porras what the HR Manager had told me. He also showed disbelief and certain nonconformity. That evening, we were going to Caracas to spend the weekend with Melody's brother and wife. We came back on Monday, and I was called again to the HR manager's office. The manager told me that he had reversed the decision and that I was to return to Caracas. My heart sunk into my stomach out of shock and disbelief. The manager told me that I should not have told anyone the news of the extension of my contract, which was apparently a secret between me and the manager. I told him that he had not asked me to keep it as a secret. The manager told me that I was expected to exercise discretion. I told the manager that I did not know the reason why he had reversed his decision before forty-eight hours had passed but that I would abide by it and prepare myself to go. I left the office of the manager and broke the bad news to Melody, but she was calm and handled it well with the children when they came back from school. Ranya was sad to leave her friends.

I made fast preparations for my return to Caracas. Fortunately, my brother in-law could rent an apartment for us in Caracas. All our Indian friends were surprised but were sympathetic. We sold both cars and some furniture. We went to the school and got the transfer certificates for the children. We went to all the restaurants we liked for a last time around. The truck came to pack our belongings. The night before our departure, the same group that welcomed us to the island gave us a farewell dinner. The next morning, all of them turned up at the airport to wish us goodbye. Joy, Ranya's best friend, and her parents were there too. I had to pull Ranya away from Joy when the last security call came for the flight. We took the commercial flight instead of the company flight because we had too much luggage. As the plane took off, we gave a last look at the beaches. Nobody spoke for a while until a friend from VPC came from behind and touched my shoulder. I had worked with him a few years before. He said he had come to the island refinery to do some trouble shooting and was returning to Caracas. He told me that he had heard about an imminent investigation on corruption charges against the managers and their expatriate accomplices. I told him that I expected such an investigation, and it was long overdue. He said that he had heard about my case and was sympathetic. We talked the whole way until the plane landed. My brother in-law was waiting at the airport. The next morning I went to the office, and I was assigned the same room I had left two years earlier. All my colleagues were still there, and they welcomed me back. I went to meet with the new HR Manager in Caracas, who was a friend of mine, and he too welcomed me back. The manager also mentioned to me about the investigation that was going to be carried out in the island refinery for corruption charges. I left the office that day wondering what I would do with the children's education. I was sure that when God closed one door, He always opened another. I had to figure out where the open door was.

CHAPTER THIRTEEN

The Farc on Our Heels

The next day, we went to the school where our children had studied before they left for the Bon Bini Island. The principal told us that there was no place either for Rajeev or Ranya. We discussed with the Principal the case of Roshni, and he told us that no school would give admission to her since she had already finished eleventh grade, which is the last grade of the Venezuelan high school system. He advised us to get a high school equivalency from the Ministry of Education. Without this equivalency, she could not get admission in any of the Venezuelan universities. She could not get admission in American universities either, since she did not have a high school diploma. We could not afford to send her to any of the two the American schools in Caracas to finish the twelfth grade. Our only alternative was to find a school with twelfth grade that was affordable to us. Years ago, the daughter of one of our Indian friends had attended an American school in a town called Rubio, near the Colombian border of

Venezuela. We called up this friend and asked details about the school. We called the school and explained our case. The Principal invited us to visit the school with the children for an interview. We drove for twelve hours and reached the school. The authorities received us kindly and provided us with accommodation in the school guests' quarters. The school was called Jansen Academy and was founded around 50 years earlier by several Evangelical missionaries, working in South America. The school was intended for the education of their children, and it came with boarding and lodging facilities. The school was obliged to give admission to a certain number of local children in order to comply with the government regulations. Our children were interviewed first, and then we were interviewed. The authorities explained to us all the rules and regulations. The payments were reasonable and affordable. After the interview, we were given a guided tour of the facilities. There were no children in the school as it was closed for the annual vacations. We liked the school but were not sure if the children would get admission. Should the admission be given, we were clueless as to whether we should leave them in the boarding. We did not have any other alternative either in our mind. We were afraid that our children would be converted to evangelism. Our suspicion was based on the fact that the Principal had uttered a few words against the Pope during our interview. In any case, we had to wait for the school to make the decision. We returned to Caracas after spending two days in Rubio.

My brother from Coral Springs, Florida called me up and asked me to go there to see if the children could get admitted into the local high school. Since I did not have any firm alternative, I thought I would give a try to his proposal. I made a reservation for the whole family to go to Miami. The day we were to travel, a hurricane hit the Venezuelan coast, and the plane could not take off. We traveled after two days and reached Coral Springs. The children were tested for English and academic proficiency. In the evening, I went to see a lawyer to find out the requirements for immigration to the US for the whole family. We told the lawyer that we were trying to get the children admitted to a US school. The lawyer pointed out that what we were trying to do was illegal. We did not know that it was illegal to study in US schools as tourists. My brother did not know it either. We dropped the whole scheme right away. At that point, we did not have any other firm alternative. When we were sitting silent and lost, a call came from Rubio. The Principal was on the other end. He said he was calling to give us the good news that all our three children were admitted to the school. He also asked me to pass by the school to make arrangements for their admission in the boarding as well. He gave the account number for some money to be deposited for tuition and boarding for the first month. I thanked the Principal and put down the telephone. We were overjoyed to know that, at last, we had somewhere to take our children. We understood then where God had opened the door for us.

We returned to Caracas, and all of us went to Rubio the next day. We had decided to rent a house near the school so that the children could attend from home. Melody offered to be with the children while I continued working in Caracas. I told the Principal of our decision to live in a rented house and let the children attend the school as day scholars, to which he finally acceded after initial resistance. We went around looking for a house for rent, when suddenly we came across a house for sale two streets in front of the school. We went into it and fell in love with it right away. We negotiated the price and left a check as part of the initial. We decided to sign the final papers the Friday before the reopening of the school. We went back to Caracas and made preparations to move to Rubio. We bought a used car for Melody and the children. I hired a truck to carry all our personal belongings that had come from the island, along with the others that were kept in storage, to be taken to Rubio. On Thursday, we drove to Rubio but could not cover the twelve hours the same day and so had to stay overnight in a hotel. On Friday, we were punctual at the Office of Registration to sign the papers and make the final payments. All went well, and by noon, the truck was unloading our belongings in the house. The children walked to the school to meet other children who had already arrived. Then, surprisingly, Ranya met Joy, her friend from the island, who came running to meet her. She, too, had left the island, as her parents were reassigned to work in a remote part of Venezuela. She had joined the school the day before. Ranya and Joy came running to the house to let us know that they both were to study together again. It was a pleasant surprise for all of us. We met Joy's parents who were staying in the school guest house. I had only the week-end to settle down Melody and the children, as I had to return to Caracas for work on Monday. We moved fast to get everything organized. We got a carpenter to fix some of the furniture that needed repair due to moving. The house had four bedrooms, and so all the children could get their own room. There was an attached party room for feasts. The whole house was enclosed by four walls with sufficient green area within to walk around. The design of the house was what caught our attention and finally made us buy it. It was a dream house. Too bad, that I was not going to live there, except on weekends. Saturday was spent shopping for food and fixing the house. The teachers brought us food on Friday, Saturday, and Sunday, so that we did not have to cook at home. That was a pleasant surprise and very kind on their part. We felt welcomed. The children made several friends, and they started coming to the house, a practice that would continue throughout our stay in Rubio. In the future, a wave of students would enter the house and disappear after drinking soda or water, or munching something light. The children enjoyed having a lot of friends.

On Sunday, we went to the local Church for mass. The Church looked like a renovated cathedral. The story goes that it was an old and small Church until an ex-president, who was from Rubio, decided to renovate it. The villagers told me that there was another Church, which was smaller, also renovated by the same person, but for his wife. Another person noted that the bigger Church was for the ex-president to pray and the smaller one for his wife to pray. Whatever reason he had to renovate the two Churches, added a bystander, he possibly would end up stealing heaven too, since he was considered one of the most corrupt presidents of Venezuela. Anyway, after mass, we decided to see the other Church too, which was small but had a feminine touch and looked better decorated.

On Monday morning, I decided not to fly back to Caracas for work since I did not want to miss my children's first day at school. I called the office and explained the reason for my absence. The reopening went very well, and the children walked home for lunch, full of news and comments. They loved everything about the school. The school continued in the afternoon until 4 PM. The most wonderful part of it was that they had to walk just two minutes to the school. No more driving to school, no more traffic, and no more late lunches. It was too good to be true. I thought of the door that was shut two months earlier in the island and of the door now wide open in Rubio. But there was a dark line to the white clouds. I knew that the Colombian border was not safe for foreigners. My family was more vulnerable without my presence. Extortion and kidnapping were an everyday business in the Colombian border towns by the leftist guerillas (FARC). They were against Christian missionaries and had kidnapped and killed some of them in the past. They could easily confuse us as missionaries or their associates. I did not mention my worry to Melody, lest she would panic and the whole project would have to be abandoned. Fortunately, the house had all the normal security devices already installed. All the four walls were quite high. The doors were fortified with iron bars. Still, I suffered internally for having to leave the family behind. I drove to San Cristobal, the capital of the state an hour away, and bought two Alsatian dogs, one male and the other female. The male was already six months old and of certified pedigree. The female was a puppy. The male dog was majestic looking, and his registered name was Askan. We kept his name. The female dog was named Milly. Both of them instantly became favorites of the children. They had enough place to run around. They were let lose at night, and they went around the house. Askan's bark was deafening. I shared my apprehensions with the Principal for leaving my family behind. The Principal said that the community would watch for their safety. That night, I did not sleep well. Early morning, the taxi came, and I woke up the children to say goodbye. My heart was pounding, but I did not show any sign of sadness or nervousness on my face. The poker face in me took control of me. I kissed Melody and the children goodbye and the taxi drove me off to the nearest airport. I did not look behind, neither did I cry in front of the taxi driver. But my heart was full of tears. I reached Caracas and went straight to the office and worked the whole day with a heavy heart.

I waited for Friday evening to take the flight back to Rubio. I reached before dark. I felt so good to be with my own and Askan and Milly. The dogs were doing fine; they had adapted to the house very well. Askan knew his responsibility, analyzed everyone who looked suspicious and barked at those who didn't look friendly. Milly played with him a lot, and he was very kind and understanding to her. Rajeev took personal care of the dogs. He even told me that he was going to be a veterinary doctor to take care of dogs. When I told him that, as a vet doctor, he would have to take care of other animals too, he kept thinking. I made use of the weekend to take the family for shopping, fixing things at home and making up the lost time for bonding. I got a gardener to pull out all the weeds from the grass and plant some saplings. The gardener told me that he had known the couple from whom the previous owner had bought the house. He added that the lady had died in the house, and the husband sold the house for a reduced price. I returned the next weekend too, and Melody told me that she heard strange noises from the kitchen side at night, but on inspection there was nothing unusual. She told me that one night there was a big noise, and she got up to look and found Rajeev standing in the dining area with a kitchen knife in his hand. He had heard too the noise and thought it was somebody breaking into the house. They inspected and found out that the bookshelf in Ranya's room had fallen down, and she was not even aware of it. Ranya could sleep like a cold stone. I never told them until we left Rubio what the gardener had told me. If I had done so, our adventure in Rubio would have come to an end as Melody believed in ghosts and was very scared of them. I was sure the children too were afraid of them. Again my poker face saved us. The weekend went very fast, and before I knew it, it was time to return to Caracas. I took the flight back on Sunday evening and reached Caracas after two hours. If I had taken the bus, I would have reached the next morning. I took the flight many times during the three years my family stayed in Rubio. But there were times I had to take the bus because I could not afford the flights or could not get reservations. The bus journey was an ordeal which only a person with absolute necessity could endure.

Rubio is a town located in the State of Tachira, on the eastern part of the Andes Mountains, around 850 meters high from the sea level. It is surrounded by hills and tropical vegetation. The main cultivation around Rubio is coffee. The temperature varies from 14 to 24 degrees centigrade. When we were there, the population was around 50,000. The capital of Tachira is San Cristobal, a town of around 500,000 people. The nearest Colombian town is Cucuta, which is 36 KM away. The road to San Cristobal is mountainous and gets blocked very often due to mud slides. The road to San Antonio where the nearest airport is located is in better condition. Cucuta is on the other side of the river from San Antonio. There is free access up to Cucuta, and we used to go there for shopping and sightseeing. The exchange rate at the time was favorable for shopping in Colombia.

In Caracas, I had the whole apartment to myself, and I hated to be alone. I moved in with a retired Spanish doctor who was eccentric. He was always in the apartment and watched every one of my moves. He complained about everything: that the juice carton in the fridge was not properly kept, too much noise while shutting the door, entering the kitchen at odd hours, etc. One day, when I came back unexpectedly from work to pick up something important from my room, I found the doctor without his wig. I didn't even know that he was wearing a wig. He did not like that I discovered him bald. His complaints increased, and he became intolerable. He objected to Melody coming to visit me. We both got tired of each other, and I moved out. I rented a room in the apartment of a lady, old enough to be my mother. She was a widow. She rented out two rooms in order to get some income which helped her meet both ends. She was of German descent but born and brought up in Venezuela. She had a brother living nearby but was not in speaking terms with him. The other room was rented to a boy who worked with the Miss Venezuela pageant as a physical trainer. He looked gay and acted like one, but I had no proof for that. He appeared one day in the apartment with five girls who were preparing for the Miss Venezuela contest. All of them were stunning. I felt very much at home in the house of the old lady. She was very accommodating when Melody came to visit me with the children. Ranya even slept in her bed.

The travels to Rubio and back were, more often than not, by overnight bus. Many times, the bus would break down on the road in the middle of nowhere at night. Fortunately, the buses that came behind took a few passengers each, but we had to stand all the way as all the seats were occupied. Sometimes, I stood for eight hours. I had no choice; either I rode standing or stayed in the street in pitch dark. Once, the bus could not proceed as the road was completely blocked by a mud slide. I had to cross a fast-running stream with my luggage on my shoulder and reach the other side of the mudslide to take another bus to continue the journey. The most annoying experience was the National Guards who would stop the bus and wake us up in the middle of the night in order to check if we were carrying drugs. The route was used by drug traffickers from Colombia. Sometimes, the National Guards checked even into the underwear. Ladies were stripped naked and checked. Melody hated bus travels mostly for this reason. During one of my visits to Rubio, Rajeev and Ranya had dental appointments to tighten their braces. I took a Monday off to take them to San Cristobal to get the dental work done, which was finished by 6 PM. I put them into a mini-bus to Rubio, and I took the night bus to Caracas. I was feeling nervous all the time that the children were traveling alone for the first time, and I prayed to their Guardian Angels to protect them. Midway, the children's bus could not proceed as there was a mudslide and the road was blocked. The driver of the bus asked all the passengers to get down and went to his house nearby. Rajeev and Ranya were stranded on the mountainous road. They did not know anyone in the bus and there was no telephone nearby to call home. At that time, a man came and introduced himself as our neighbor, the one who lived in front of our house in Rubio. The children did not know him, but he said he had seen them. He said he was driving to Rubio through a roundabout way and that they were welcome to ride with him. They trusted him and accepted his offer and reached home three hours later to Melody, who was totally worried, not knowing what had happened to her children. When I returned to Rubio, I went to the house of the neighbor and thanked him for being the Guardian Angel for my children. You see prayers are heard, and miracles do happen. The children were vulnerable; anything could have happened to them, but their Guardian Angels protected them.

We were afraid that our children were targets for conversion. We explained to them the reasons we were Catholics and told them that their religion was not negotiable. We also told them not to get into any discussion over religion with anyone in the school, or confront anyone talking bad of the Pope or the Catholic Religion, and that they should respect the religion of everyone. Our advice stood them in good stead, and no dent had been made to their faith. By the way, I believe that people of all religions can live together; worshiping one God they all believe, in their own way. All religions are faith-based, and since none of them are scientifically proven, all are equally valid. If this mental attitude can be achieved, we can learn to live side-by-side with persons of other religions. It is arrogance to think that our faith is the only right faith, especially when we have nothing other than faith to prove it. This does not mean that we should treat our faith lightly. We can be serious with our own faith and at the same time respect the seriousness of other people's faith too. If we are convinced about the message of our faith and want other people to have the same message, be a living example of it. That is the best way and perhaps the only way of preaching the message of our religion that will convince other people. Preaching without example is a lie and a disservice to our religion. Violence can never be an instrument of conversion; in fact, it will drive people away from our religion. May we be living examples of our religion and let other people see God from our works.

Jansen Academy was a model institution for teaching and learning. It was very active in sports and extracurricular activities. It lived and taught Christian and civic values. I could see the progress of my children every time I visited Rubio. I could see their knowledge increasing and new skills developing. The school offered them the chance to participate in many extracurricular activities that gave them the opportunity to acquire and practice many academic and life skills. There were abundant opportunities for sports like basketball, football (soccer), and other games. Every Saturday afternoon was reserved for football competition. Teams from around the area were invited to play with the Jansen Academy team. Rajeev played for the soccer team. Likewise, every

Sunday was reserved for basket-ball competition. The school conducted streets cleanup campaign wherein both students and teachers participated. The students visited prisons to entertain the prisoners, visited poor people's houses to help in whatever way they could, and went to hospitals to do voluntary service. The school conducted several fundraiser drives to generate money for their social service programs. Children were baking cakes at home for sale, making decorations for a reception, or conducting donations drive for a good cause. My children were so busy with so many activities that some days we did not even see them except for moments. Some time they were gone for the entire week-end. We did not worry about them, even though they were at the Colombian border because they were well accompanied by teachers. We felt as if we ended up in the Promised Land. We are eternally thankful to Jansen Academy for the opportunity to educate our children there. One of the teachers that truly deserved our admiration was Joan Siena. She had the tremendous capacity to motivate children to perform their best. She was there twenty-four hours to help them with whatever problems they had. Joan was a model to imitate, a true teacher and an inspiration. I do not even remember what subject she taught my children, but they consulted her for practically every subject. Ranya kept in touch with her for many years, but lately have lost trace of her. Wherever she is, let her know how much we appreciate her for what she has done for our children. She has definitely played a very important part in their development. Joan will be remembered for a long time in our family.

Roshni graduated from the twelfth grade and got admitted at Rutgers University in New Jersey, USA. It was the first graduation in our family and her godfather, Eduardo, came especially to accompany her for the joyful occasion. I bought a camcorder and took several scenes of the graduation ceremony and the feast that followed. The next day, we left for India for vacations. On the way, we visited Paris, using the time share we had bought in Orlando. We had reserved an apartment in Paris, starting on a Friday. We reached Charles de Gaulle airport at 8 PM. We were five, and the taxis took no more than four people according to the law. We were looking for a bigger car to no avail. Although I had four years of French in college, I could not understand it, let alone speak it. I decided to take two taxis, Melody and two children in one and I and one child in the other. But, being so late, I was afraid to trust the immigrant drivers, especially since we were traveling in separate cars. Fortunately, both drivers coordinated very well in the Paris traffic and reached the building at the same time. I gave a sigh of relief. But, when we tried to enter the resort hotel, the door was locked. The receptionist had gone home. Just then, one of the residents came out, and I and the children went in. We looked around, and there was an envelope at the reception desk with my name and the keys for the apartment in it. I again gave a sigh of relief, and the drivers accompanied us to the apartment. They took our luggage up and made sure that everything functioned. I really appreciated their help and reserved them for the return journey one week later. I was sorry, initially, I was not comfortable with the taxi drivers because they were immigrants from Nigeria, but they turned out to be excellent people. I wished I could have been free of prejudice and suspicion, but my priority at that moment was the safety of my family.

We spent one week in Paris and visited almost all the monuments, however brief it was. We were really impressed by the art and sculptures in every nook and corner of the city. The bridges are so artistically carved. The Eiffel Tower, the Cathedral of Notre Dame, the Tomb of Napoleon Bonaparte, the Opera House, the Madeleine Church, Champs-Elysees, and the Louvre Museum are some of the landmarks, among others, that captured our memory. We also visited the Versailles Palace outside Paris. Ranya took notes of all the monuments, and they have been the theme of several essays that she wrote during her school studies. We noticed that the McDonalds hamburger was smaller than its equivalent in the US. It may be related to the fact that French people eat smaller portions. At the end of the week, we called the taxi drivers, and they took us back to the airport. We left for London to catch the British Airways flight to Bombay. We vowed to return to Paris, for we left so much more to see. We were not satisfied with the time spent in some of them. One week is too short to see Paris.

We were visiting India for the first time after the death of Melody's father, and his absence was very much felt. Both of our mothers were in good health. We flew to Delhi and visited the Taj Mahal, which impressed all of us. I was visiting it the second time. We flew to London and checked into a hotel. When we sneezed, dark soot was coming out of our noses, for the air pollution of New Delhi was very high. The buses and taxis in New Delhi have been converted to run on natural gas since then, and so the pollution is very much controlled at present. We spent three days in London for some sightseeing, but Ranya fell sick of stomach trouble; she also developed skin sores due to mosquito and other insect's bites in India. She was treated by a doctor and went along with the visits. We saw Westminster Abbey, The Houses of Parliament, Big Ben, Buckingham Palace, Hyde Park, the Tower of London, and Saint Paul's Cathedral. All the monuments and landmarks were very impressive. We returned to Rubio after being away for a month.

I took Roshni to Rutgers for a one-week orientation program before classes started. We toured the campus, registered for the courses, paid the fees, opened an account in the bank for Roshni, got her admitted to a hostel for girls, and introduced her to some freshmen. Most of her classes were at the Engineering campus. I told both my brothers in New York to take care of her and left for Venezuela. The tuition and hostel fees were sent directly to the university. I left some pocket money for her to spend. When I returned after one semester, I saw that the pocket money was almost intact. When I asked her why she had not used her pocket money, she said she didn't need to buy anything. When I asked if she did not buy her cosmetics, she said that she waited for me to come and buy for her. She was always very cautious about spending money.

I sent Rajeev for a crash course in SAT to the house of my brother in Coral Springs, during Christmas vacations. He scored well in the exam. During the spring break, the whole family went to Coral Springs and participated in the baptism of my niece. I was asked to be her godfather, and I gladly accepted it.

After the feast, we went up to Punta Gorda on the west coast of Florida, where we had a reservation in a time-share resort. Roshni came down from New Jersey for the baptism and to be with us at the resort. We had a wonderful time at the beach and visited several places of interest in and around Tampa. We flew to New York to visit my two brothers and to visit Rutgers, where Rajeev was to start studies in the following fall. Initially, he was to study vet medicine, but later on he switched to Animal Husbandry. While we were driving through the Cooks campus, I saw a big board on which was written, "Nabisco Food Science Department". The building looked impressive, and I told Roshni to look into Food Science as her major. I thought Rutgers was strong in Food Science, judging from the buildings and the bill-board of Nabisco; I thought the Food Science Department was well-funded that there wouldn't be a shortage of jobs in this area, as people always needed to eat. We looked around for a school for Ranya to study, as we planned to move to the US in the fall. We finally selected the East Brunswick High School, New Jersey, as we were told that this school was better known and very much respected in the community. Ranya was to study the eleventh and twelfth grades. We consulted with a student counselor to find out if the school would admit a foreign student. The counselor told us that we had to be residents of the area to qualify for admission and that the school would have to issue an I-20 form for Ranya to apply for a student visa at the American Consulate in Caracas. We decided to rent an apartment in the area to comply with the residency requirement when the time came for admission for Ranya. We returned to Rubio, and life continued as before.

Pope John Paul II was coming to Barinas, a city four-hour's drive from Rubio, to inaugurate a new Basilica of our Lady of Coromoto, declared by the Government as the Patron of Venezuela. The Basilica was constructed at the very sight where she is said to have appeared to a Red Indian boy. The design and construction costs were entirely borne by the government. Melody, me, and Ranya, went to visit the Basilica. We reached the night before, took a room in a hotel, and visited the site before the Pope and the crowed arrived the next day. Rajeev stayed back at home as he had to practice for a play in the school during that weekend. I had to park the car far away, but there was a shuttle bus between the parking lot and the Basilica. There were a lot of people even that early for the Pope's arrival. Many slept in the field. The Basilica was beautiful. When we were trying to get into the shuttle to get back to the parking lot, some men suddenly decided to get out of the bus (who actually had got in first), creating an unnecessary commotion. I wondered what the objective of this commotion was. We went straight to a restaurant as we were very hungry; and when the time came to pay the bill, there was no money in my pocket. I was pick-pocketed by the men who created the commotion in the bus. This is a usual trick that is played to pick-pocket people: create a commotion in which one is subjected to some physical constraints, and one's attention is diverted into liberating oneself from the discomfort, during which time, the thieves pick-pocket. Fortunately, I had some money in the purse. I felt stupid for having kept the money loosely in the pant pocket. This was a lesson for me. From then onwards, I divided the money between

Melody and me during travels. We went back to the Basilica the next day early morning to see the Pope and participate in his mass. He came on time and toured on an open car so that all the people could see him. When he appeared, all the people burst into applause. His cheeks looked red because of the intense heat of Barinas. We returned to Rubio in the afternoon, but had hardly enough cash to buy gasoline. The Evangelists in Rubio teased me, saying I had gone to confess to the Pope.

The graduation of Rajeev was around the corner, and everyone got excited for the second graduation in the family. He went to Aruba for the senior trip and came back with some skin loss from the hands and feet. He fell down from the motor bike that he was riding for the first time. He learnt his lesson the hard way and never touched a motor bike again. The graduation ceremony was simple but inspiring. The Principal gave a speech that touched the hearts of all present. A family lunch was organized at Caldero, a popular local restaurant for Spanish food.

I had all the plans made to move Melody and the children to the US. I was to continue working in Caracas. We got an apartment rented in Roshni's name, in the East Brunswick area. We bought an apartment in Caracas and moved there with all our belongings from Rubio. We closed the house in Rubio and left it with a real estate agent for sale. The dogs were given away to a person who wanted them to guard his estate. We felt very bad to send the dogs away, especially for Rajeev, who was their guardian. Rajeev and Ranya were issued visas from the US Consulate in Caracas. We landed at the Kennedy Airport on the 16th of August, 1996.

Roshni had stayed back in the university as she took some summer courses.

Unfortunately, Jansen Academy had to be closed down five years after our children graduated. The FARC was closing in on the school. It was truly risky to operate the school, and the authorities decided to close it. When a good school like Jansen Academy cannot operate in a democratic country, it speaks volumes of the state of affairs of that country. Fortunately, the authorities could see what was coming, and took measures to avoid tragedies waiting to happen. The FARC was practically at our heels, and we got out of Rubio on time. Congratulations to the Jansen Academy for the fifty years of dedicated service in the formation of thousands of students from all over the world.

CHAPTER FOURTEEN

The New Jersey Connection

We stayed in one of the Pocono's mountains resorts in Pennsylvania using the time-share, and commuted every day to and from the university for the orientation program for Rajeev. During the program, he selected the courses he wanted to study for the first semester. One of the courses was Animal Care, as he had in mind specializing in Animal Husbandry. We also completed all the paper work for Ranya's admission at East Brunswick High School, New Jersey. The apartment was handed over to us, and we moved in. We slept on the floor for four days, as the apartment came with no furniture, and all the furniture shops were closed for the Labor Day weekend. On the fifth day, we bought some used furniture and U-hauled them to the apartment. It felt good sleeping on a bed again. We bought a used car and called a driving school to teach Roshni. She was quick to learn and passed the driver's test and started driving to college with Rajeev. Not very long after, Rajeev also got his driver's license and started driving the car. One of the practical for the animal care course for Rajeev was a bath to a cow. After the practical, he decided that he did not want to continue any more with the Animal Husbandry major. He thought of specializing in arts and so took a course on drawing for the second semester. He was asked to draw the figure of a nude woman with a live model in front of him, which left him traumatized and that was the end of the art specialty, too. Finally, he ended up specializing in economics with a minor in accounting.

My vacation was over, and I returned to Caracas, after settling down Melody and children in East Brunswick. Melody had to stay back as the authorities of East Brunswick High School required that one of the parents stayed with Ranya, a minor. Initially, I felt very lonely in the apartment. At times, I used to shout the names of Melody and the children to the four walls just to get rid of my nostalgia for them. My lonely life went on for two years, except for the fifteen days of vacation in summer and another fifteen days in December that I spent with the family. When my family was in Rubio, I could see them at least once in fifteen days. Now, I could see them only once in six months. My phone bill sky-rocketed for all the calls I made to New Jersey. But we were happy that the children were getting a good education. A lot of things were happening in my office that affected me. All affiliates of VPC were put together as one company. Every one became direct employees of VPC. Training functions from all the companies were put together, and that meant movement of people from buildings and offices. Just like training, all the functional departments were put together, and people, who were so far rivals, were asked to work together. This was done without previous consultation or preparation. The whole thing was welcomed with reluctance as something forced upon. It was not a smooth transition. Many people ended up for some time not knowing what office to go or what they were supposed to do. Some of them stared at each other still as rivals, unwilling to share information. For example, the exploration people from different companies had data on their areas which they did not want to share with colleagues of other companies, even though they were asked to explore all areas together. The process of integration took a long time to sink into the employees. The mind-set had to be rewired, and this took its own course to set.

I had a health problem which I had not shared with my family, and I revealed it to them when I was at home in New Jersey for vacations. It happened this way: one day, after breakfast, I felt very tired and I had to take to bed. My head was reeling. It was a strange feeling and not easily described. I felt like throwing myself out through the window. There was a feeling of pain: physical, mental, emotional, and even existential. I thought of the boy in Maracay who threw himself out through the balcony from the thirteenth floor. When I thought of Melody and the children, I felt the responsibility of caring for them. When I thought of God, I knew that all lives are His and He is the only one free to dispose it off. I held on to the bed so that I didn't even get up. This fit of breakdown had happened to me two times earlier. As described before, the first time happened on the way back from India after leaving Melody and Roshni. I checked into a hotel in New York and slept for twenty-four hours. When I woke up, my flight was gone, but I had gotten over the problem. The second time happened in Caracas, in our apartment. I did not give Melody and the children any hint; I told them that I was tired and took to bed. A twenty-four hours rest in bed cured the disease. This was the third time. I knew more or less when it was coming. I now think, in all the three instances, it was a nervous breakdown because it was preceded by very stressful events. Thank God I survived all the three episodes. It hasn't been repeated to this day. I cannot imagine what could have happened if it had come when I was alone and depressed on the fifth floor of the apartment in Caracas.

There were two guys in my office who were known to be gay, called Carlos and Oscar. They remained bachelors, although according to tradition, they had already passed the age of marriage. Both were very nice individuals, very pleasant to deal with. One day, Carlos was stabbed by a person whom he had contracted for painting the apartment. Apparently, they had a discussion. Carlos pretended to be dead and, so the assailant left him. The neighbor lady heard his cry and called the police, who opened the apartment and took him to the hospital. I visited him in the hospital and Carlos told me his version of what had happened. He recuperated and was back for work. I suspected that the painter actually was his gay partner. The suspicion arose because one month later, Oscar was strangled in his apartment by his gay partner. We were very sad for what happened to Oscar and accompanied him to his grave. Not too long after, Carlos was diagnosed with AIDS, and we had to take precautions when we shook hands with him. He started to be absent from work, and his health deteriorated rapidly. He went on a tour of Europe and came back to be hospitalized. He died quietly and left all who knew him perplexed about the destiny of life. Two lives ended suddenly, violently, and prematurely. They could have had a better end, but who is to be blamed for their premature departure? They say we live the choices we make; but, are we free to make those choices? Were they gay from free choice or did they inherit the genes to be gay? Life sometimes baffles us. We wish we had answers.

Roshni enjoyed her studies as a Food Science major. She had good professors and made good grades at the end, although she had difficulties in the beginning. She graduated and got a job with a flavor company. She continued her studies to the Masters, and the company helped her with the tuition. I took the three children to Atlantic City for a week, as part of Roshni's graduation celebration, using the time-share facility. Melody had gone to India for the marriage of her niece. Only Roshni was allowed into the Casinos. The other two were caught and warned by the security for playing the machines. Two days into the vacation, we were woken up during the middle of the night three times by the fire alarm. We had to rush down from the twentieth floor through the freezing cold outside in the iron stairs, only to find out that it was a hoax played by three African American children staying in the hotel. We left the next day to Chicago to visit some relatives. Our visit got frozen again by a blizzard that left twenty-three inches of snow in the drive-way. We had to dig out our car for the return journey.

We bought a townhouse in East Brunswick, which the children liked very much. They got a young border collie to accompany them, but it was too strong for them to handle and they gave it away. They then got a Dobson, which fitted all their needs, and he is presently the most loved dog in the world. The children and their friends got together very often to have a barbeque at home. Ranya walked to her school.

We planned to get together in December, 1999 to celebrate Christmas in Caracas. Roshni and Ranya landed on the 14th night, and Melody and I went to pick them up at the airport amidst pouring rain. We rushed back to Caracas through the climbing and winding freeway, fearing that the road could be blocked by mudslides. Fortunately, we reached home after driving a lot longer, still raining. In the morning, the TV stations announced that two mudslides occurred after we had passed. Several cars and people were trapped between the two mudslides. The children recognized two ladies who were sitting by their side in the plane, among the trapped passengers. One of them was invalid and was on crutches. The government airlifted the passengers to safety, but they had to go through many ordeals. Rajeev was to come two days later due to exams. The heavy rain continued into 16th morning, when the side facing the Caribbean Sea of the Avila Mountain (not the side facing Caracas) gave way, originating a huge landslide which got converted into several mudslides. These mudslides rushed down the mountain, carrying heavy stones that rumbled through several rivers that over-boarded and carried several houses and people to the sea. Thirty thousand lives were lost, and there were much damage to properties and loss of personal possessions. The airport was not affected, but it was closed for commercial traffic as it was fully used for relief operations. All the flights were diverted to nearby airports. Many flights, including that of Rajeev, were cancelled. Finally, after spending forty-eight hours between his uncle's house in Queens and JFK, he boarded a plane that took him to another airport two hours from Caracas. Thank God he was able to reach before Christmas. But, the Christmas spirit was lost because of the tragedy. The return flight was from Caracas airport, as things had settled down by then.

At the fourth year of Rajeev's college, he was admitted for practical training under my investment banker. He was assigned the job of marketing the financial investment products offered by the bank. He learned a lot during the training, which lasted six full months. After he had graduated, he was offered a job in the same bank. I am proud of my boy, who could not even maintain good attention in class as a child and became a priced employee of a banking institution. I have to acknowledge the help that my broker rendered to get my son admitted for training, supervising his work and finally recommending him for a job in his company. Later, I found out that my investment banker was making more money for himself than for me. I used to follow the Wall Street and saw the prices of so many shares going up and so many people making so much money. I decided to take control of my portfolio and make the investments myself. I bought some technology shares that were hyped up by investment advisors from Wall Street. I made 30,000 on paper in two months. That was not bad, and encouraged by the bonanza, I borrowed some money from my account and invested in some more shares. I made some more money and waited the shares to go up more before selling and cashing in. And then suddenly, the internet bubble burst on Wall Street and my shares were the first to tumble because they were the most risky. In two days, I lost all the profits I had made and even started losing the capital. Hope is the last to be lost in Las Vegas, and so it was in Wall Street for unseasoned investors. I hoped that the market would turn around, and the value of my shares would recuperate. The shares never turned around and even got worse after the 9/11 terrorist attack. I lost almost all my investments. My quest for a fast buck led me to make risky investments. I lamented that I had only sixty-four days managing my account, which I thought was a very short time to learn and experiment in Wall Street. My only consolation was that I was not the only person who lost money; every one of my friends had lost too, but not as much as I did. They were more diversified than me. I had invested wholly in technology stocks, and they were the hardest hit. Even some of my friends who had seasoned portfolio managers lost a lot of money and took more than five years to recuperate. My investments in real estate made me money and saved me from a disaster. I thanked God for having given me a soft landing. There is a saying in Spanish: "God squeezes but does not strangle". How true this is in my case!

Ranya was admitted to Bryn Mawr College in Pennsylvania. Her graduation from High School was celebrated with friends and relatives. Melody came back to Caracas after Ranya's graduation. We were not at home in New Jersey to take her to college. Kelly, a Jewish woman who lived below our apartment in East Brunswick and who became like a mother to our children, took her to college. Ranya introduced her as her other mom. She enjoyed her studies and majored in English and Political Science, with a strong orientation to journalism. I was especially impressed by the examinations and grading system in Bryn Mawr. The exams were posted on the internet and the answers could also be sent through the internet. I asked Ranya if anybody cheated by referring to books or taking more than the assigned time. She told me that there was an honor code which everybody respected. These days, in many universities in the US, questions and answers are posted online. Each question has a certain amount of time assigned for answering it, and if one goes beyond the allotted time, the answer will not be accepted. Books can be used, but the time spent on referring to books gets deducted from the time available for answering the question. How many colleges can boast of a system of exams by internet? Ranya told me that if anybody cheated, Bryn Mawr had the means of detecting it, thus making it a full-proof system.

One day, Ranya called us in Caracas to inform that Joy had drowned along with two other friends on a beach in Mexico. Joy was studying in Birmingham, Alabama and had gone to Mexico with a group of people in an Evangelical mission. The under-current carried two of them into the deep, and their bodies were washed on to the beach the next day. Ranya flew to Birmingham, for the arrival of the body and took part in the burial. She came back completely shaken up and emotionally shattered. She took her time to get healed. Bad news kept coming. On 11th September, 2001 morning, when Melody returned from her walk at 9.00 AM, she saw on TV that a plane had hit one of the World Trade towers in Manhattan. She immediately called me and appraised me of what was happening. Soon, I got another call from her saying that another plane had struck, and it was suspected to be a terrorist attack. She called again to confirm that it was indeed a terrorist attack as the Pentagon building in Washington had also been hit. Then we recollected that Rajeev used to go to the World Trade Center for meetings. We started searching for him and finally got word from one of his friends that he was safe and sound. A few people from his company were attending a breakfast in one of the towers for which Rajeev was not invited, and all of them died. Soon, he called back to let us know that he was fine and that he was not anywhere near the World Trade Center when it was hit. We gave a sigh of relief and thanked God for sparing our son.

Ranya progressed very much at Bryn Mawr. She did three summer internships: the first one in Saveur Magazine in New York City, the second in ABC Washington D.C, and the third in CNN in Spanish, also in Washington D.C. In ABC, she directly worked with a famous journalist in his program called Nightline. She also enjoyed working with CNN in Spanish, and made many lasting friends. She enjoyed journalism, and she took all the courses needed to have a good standing in the subject between Bryn Mawr, Haverford, and Upenn. The graduation of Ranya from Bryn Mawr was attended by all her uncles and her friends of the school days. Kelly and her husband Kenny were present too. The graduation day was doubly sweet because the previous day, she had been called by one of the TV networks and offered a job as production journalist. Her summer internships stood her in good stead. On graduation day, all her professors were happy for her that she had found the ideal job.

We were planning to visit India for the marriage of our niece. The day we were to leave NJ, a tsunami struck South East Asia, India, and Sri Lanka. We were afraid that our flight would get cancelled, but fortunately, the flight took off, and we reached Kuwait. The connecting flight to Bombay was cancelled due to technical problems, according to the airline. We were put up in a hotel in Kuwait, and, we flew to Bombay the next day. We missed the connecting flight and missed a part of the marriage ceremonies. After the marriage, we made our usual pilgrimage to Velankanni, the shrine of the Blessed Virgin which got a direct hit by the tsunami. We saw with our own eyes all the destruction it had left. We also heard accounts of people who were affected by the tsunami. When the tsunami struck, ten of my cousins were visiting the shrine. Eight of them were inside the Church attending mass, and the other two were outside the Church shopping souvenirs. All the people inside the Church were saved, as not a drop of water entered it. The two cousins outside the Church ran and escaped. A thousand corpses were dug up from the Church premises, and many cars and tourist busses were buried in the sand. The thirty-foot waves that came through the river at the back of the Church knocked its compound walls, ran through the town, taking with it many lives and possessions. The waves that came through the front of the Church were weak and stopped at its steps. My cousins were reunited the next day at the relief center that was put up in the next town. They returned by train, as their tourist bus was lost in the sand. I was invited by the Metuchen

Diocese in New Jersey to form part of its commission to study the needs of the tsunami affected people of the Diocese of Thanjavoor, India. I travelled to India with the Commission and toured the affected areas of the Diocese, which included the Velankanni Shrine. We saw villages that had been washed out entirely; only some mud walls were left to tell the story. We recommended donations to be given by the Metuchen Diocese for the construction of 4,000 houses. They have been constructed and handed over to the affected people. Congratulations to the Metuchen and Thanjavoor Diocese for the achievement.

After the graduation of our last child, we felt that we had achieved our educational goals by getting all of them graduated from good universities in the US, which helped them land up in good jobs. We were sure that everything else would fall into place. They are in pursuit of the American dream. New Jersey became their home state. All the three of them resided there. There was no lack of opportunity to make Indian friends there. It is the state in the US with maximum population of Indian expatriates.

CHAPTER FIFTEEN

Back to River Pond

There were rumors that the government would confiscate any house other than the principal one used for living, and give it away to the poor who did not own a house. We had two apartments, a three bedroom one situated in an upper middle class section of Caracas where we lived, and a beach apartment just half an hour from the city and very near to the airport. We made plans to sell the apartment in Caracas and move to the beach house, where we thought we would be safer. We put the apartment for sale and not long after, we signed it off for a reasonable price and moved into our two bedroom beach apartment. It was situated in a new building and faced the sea. Also, there was a military barrack nearby, so we felt safe to walk around the area. We took long walks in the early morning along the beach. The airport was so nearby, we could watch the planes landing and taking off from our windows. Of course, the noise was sometimes deafening, but we got used to it; after a while we were not even aware of it.

However, we did not know what to do with our lives after my retirement, which was less than two years away. We did not know where to settle down: in the US or Venezuela or India. We did not have the proper visa required to settle down in the US and be with the children. We had gone to the US on a visitor visa every time. To stay in Venezuela was becoming more and more unsafe. Express kidnapping was becoming a way of life. One of my friends who arrived at the Caracas airport from Europe was kidnapped and left naked in a beach after he had been forced to empty his checking account through several ATMs. Leaving Venezuela was like uprooting a tree with large, wide and deep roots. We knew it was going to be very painful to leave behind a way of life we had liked very much, the many friends we had made, the many memories of raising children, the many experiences at work, the many places we had visited, the country that had welcomed us like a mother and made our stay very comfortable and happy. We had enjoyed every bit of our existence in Venezuela. We had no pains or bad memories to leave behind except the death of our first born. It was to be heart rending to leave Venezuela. By the process of discarding, we decided to settle down in India. A good part of my family was still there: five brothers, uncles, aunts, cousins, and other relatives. Melody's mother wanted her to return and settle down near her. It was not going to be easy to reintegrate into the society after thirty-eight years of absence. We did not possess a house of our own to walk into. We hadn't invested in India, as we never planned to settle down there. The pension that I would get from VPC was enough for both of us to live comfortably. We planned to settle down in Kerala, as we both were born and brought up in that state. But, where in Kerala would we settle down? Our parents' houses were five hundred miles apart. It took around twelve hours to go from one house to the other in train or by road. Melody's house was located in a town, and mine in a village; our houses were at the extremes of Kerala, which stretches from north to south. If we chose to settle down in the middle, we would be in the midst of total strangers. If we chose to settle down near either of the parents' houses, one of us would be far away from the dear ones. We decided to settle down in a place where normal conveniences of life were available. When our children and grand children would visit us, they would need to feel good at the place where we settled down. Sometimes, the decision making process can split people's heads. For many people, these types of decisions are easy to make, but for us it was difficult. The time hadn't come to make the final step yet. We were primarily going through the exercise in our heads. We hoped that when the time finally arrived, God would inspire us to make the right decision. For the time being, we only know that, one day, we have to say farewell to Venezuela and that it was going to be hard.

We decided to take a trip to India, to get an idea of possible places where we could settle down. When we reached NJ, we got a call from one of my brothers in New York, saying that my mother was seriously ill. We flew the next day and reached home to see our mother conscious but not in good health. All my brothers who lived in the US arrived the next week, thus completing all the children at her bedside—ten boys. Knowing that the death of my mother was near, I asked my son Rajeev to come and visit his grandmother for the last time. She died peacefully while both of us were on our way from the airport to her bedside. He was consoled that at least he could attend her funeral.

After a week, I went for a retreat to a place well known among Catholics of central Kerala. A retreat is a spiritual experience in a place where one is isolated from the daily routines for a certain period of time, wherein one meditates over one's life with the help of a spiritual director (usually a priest) and takes resolutions to correct what is wrong in one's life. In this process, one may attend talks on spiritual matters, go through some group exercises, participate in religious liturgies, or spend time in individual reflection and prayer. The retreat lasted one week. The participation at the retreat center was something that we had resisted for years, in spite of pressure from family members who had attended it and had recommended it. Something told me that I would not like the experience in the place that was recommended to us. Still, we checked into the room provided by the center on a Sunday afternoon. The room had minimum conveniences and was given to us only at the recommendation of our parish priest. Men and women were given accommodation in separate dormitories, but we were an exception. The first day at 6 PM we were asked to congregate in a hall where there were around five thousand participants. The chairs were so close that one had to maneuver not to touch his or her neighbor while sitting. The men were on one side and the ladies on the other. One of the priests spoke about the benefits of the retreat and how one should conduct oneself to reap the maximum benefit from the experience. The priest, however, wanted to assure that the attendants met certain conditions before the whole process began. He asked everyone who smoked beedi to stand up. I stood up even though I used to smoke it once in a while during my visit to India. I felt that everybody was looking at me. The priest asked all those who had stood up to go back to the room and bring the beedis if they had any hidden there. Some of us went back to the room and returned with their findings and deposited them at the feet of the statue of Christ while the rest of us kept standing. Then the priest allowed us to sit down. Again the priest asked everybody who drank alcohol to stand up, even those who engaged in social drinking like weekends and holidays. I stood up again as I was a social drinker and felt that I was being noticed by others again. The priest lambasted the people who were standing, pointing out how bad it was to drink, and the catastrophic consequences it brought to the individual and family. Apparently drinking was a serious problem among the people. After fifteen minutes of drilling, those who had brought bottles to the room were asked to go back and bring them and deposit them at the feet of Christ, which only one person did. Then the priest continued with the theme of the evening followed by mass. The session ended at 9.00 PM, and dinner was served. There was a long queue with people holding a plate that they picked up on the way. I too stood in the queue, and when my turn came, an attendant served some rice into my plate from a huge vessel; another poured some sambar—a loose vegetable stew—and another gave a fried sardine. We ate standing in a hall that was under repair. We had to wash the plate in the tap before throwing it into a tank. I did not eat thereafter because I felt the food, the serving process, and the environment was not hygienic enough. I drank tea in a stall within the campus and ate some biscuits while others ate their meals. It was said that nobody who ate there had fallen sick. I wondered how I would survive there for a week without eating though. The gates were closed, and no one was allowed to go out before the completion of the retreat.

A loud bell woke us up at 5.00 AM and another at 5.45 AM, beckoning us to the Church for morning talks, meditations, and liturgies. There were attendants to push us out if we were late. The morning prayers began at 6.00 AM. Breakfast was served at 8.00 AM followed by free time and then talks. Lunch was served at 2.00 PM followed by free time until 6.00 PM when the evening prayers, meditation, and liturgy began. This was the routine for the whole week. Melody became alarmed when I continued without eating until Wednesday. She requested the authorities to let me out to have a meal in one of the restaurants in town. It was the policy of the center not to allow anybody out before Saturday evening. Two years earlier, one of my cousins had jumped the walls of this center and escaped; he could not stand the cloistered life and the poor food. Melody's request was refused at first, with the observation that people from western countries should adapt to the simple life of Kerala and even be an example of simplicity to the ordinary people who attended the retreat. I argued that I was used to better hygienic conditions and that I was not feeling comfortable consuming food served in the center. After a few minutes of argument, the authorities let me out along with Melody, cautioning us not to tell anyone. We went and had a good meal in a nearby restaurant.

The overall experience at the center was positive; it made us reflect over our life and the necessary corrections we had to make. I did not like at all the shouting of halleluiah and the beating of the lips by some participants during the talks and liturgies. The testimony of cures during the health miracle session seemed dubious. The insinuation and subtle pressure to donate money left some doubts in me about the center. Christ and riches do not go together. The whole experience was a little too noisy for me. I liked the quiet environment for prayer, silence, reflection, and liturgical participation, which I had experienced in the Trapezes and Benedictine monasteries in Venezuela.

Speaking of retreats, the experience of my mother is worth mentioning. My Mother used to complain about several sicknesses, and one of them was feeling hot flashes and body itches. One neighbor lady used to advise her to go to a nearby retreat center—not the one I went to—run by nuns, pray for a cure, and donate some money. My Mother, who was very careful with spending her money, did not heed her advice at first, but one day, put a thousand rupees into her bag and asked my younger brother to leave her in the retreat center. She informed him that she was going to attend a one day retreat and that he had to pick her up on his way back. She entered the center at 10.00 AM, prayed for a while, went to the nearby hospital cafeteria for a coffee, went back to the retreat hall, and got out to reflect whether to donate money or not. Finally, after much reflection and meditation, she went to the office of the nuns and donated the money. The nun who received the money enquired about her sickness and noted it on a piece of paper. My mother went back to the hall to pray more, and within minutes, the loud speaker announced her name and declared that she has been cured of her hot flashes and body itching. She felt the response was too fast, that not enough time had elapsed for her petition to reach heaven. She did not feel the cure had occurred; she felt cheated. She got out from the retreat hall and waited for my brother to arrive. On the way home, she asked him to stop the car and explained what had happened and how she lost a thousand rupees. In those days, a thousand rupees amounted to a decent sum of money. She felt the neighbor lady was an agent of the retreat center. My brother had to console her that she meant well and that she would be rewarded one way or another for her sacrifice and that those who got the money from her have to be accountable to God. She was not convinced of his words, and felt the loss of her money for some years. By the way, the neighbor lady could not enter her house for some time. The nun and a school-teacher who were running the retreat center broke up, and the teacher set up another center across the street. There is something in the retreat that makes some people to conduct it.

We returned to Venezuela to prepare ourselves for retirement. VPC had a pre-retirement course. I was asked to attend it, as I was on the list for retirement. The course was to be given in the island of Margarita, which is considered a tropical paradise, well known for its sun and beaches. Both husband and wife were invited for the course. The participants were put up in Margarita Hilton, a five star hotel. The food was excellent. During the course, the participants were taught how to spend the time usefully during retirement, how to manage finances, how to keep good health, and above all how to enjoy life to the fullest. We were taken to beaches, visited the islands nearby, played games, and made friends with other couples. We did not know how the week had gone by before the course was over. Some of us left Margarita with the desire to return and settle down there. Back in the office, I was very much in discomfort with all the rapid changes that were taking place in VPC. All the Directors of the company were replaced, and they were political appointees. This was very much contrary to the merit system that was in place. An employee suddenly got promoted, which would have taken years according to the merit system. I said to myself that I would have to be a witness and even be part of many more such practices which I could not accept. The company was giving incentives for people close to the retirement age to take that final step. I could not let the chance go by and so opted for an early retirement. I was 58 years old, two years shy of the mandatory retirement age. Enough is enough, and I had done my part, and it was time to go home for good. I signed the retirement papers with no remorse or regrets. I went home and woke up the next day a free bird with a pension. I felt strange that I was not working and that my routine had changed. I had plenty of time on my hands and did not know what to do with it. After a few days, I started finding fault with everything that Melody was doing: the apartment was not properly organized, it was not cleaned regularly, there was dust everywhere, and the flower vases were placed in the wrong places, and so on. Suddenly, I felt that I had discovered a lot of things wrong in the house, which I had not noticed for twenty-six years.

Melody protested that I had become a critic because I did not have anything to do at home. She felt offended that, after she had run the house for so many years, I suddenly claimed that I had better ideas to organize it. It became so bad that some days I got out of the house and went off to the Office of Attention to the Retired. There, I found a number of colleagues just like me, not able to adapt to the retired life at home. One of them told me that he did not last two months at home before he got out and looked for a part time job. This left me thinking, and I too wanted something to keep myself busy. I called up some of my friends working in transnational petroleum companies, which had formed collaborative ventures with VPC to exploit hard crude. These companies were not bound by the mandatory retirement rules of the government and VPC. A friend from one of these companies called me up and offered me a job to be their training advisor. It was a full time job, and I accepted it. In my new job, I was working for a gentleman who was from Scotland called Alex. He was the finest person I had ever worked for. He was very hard working, democratic in approach, kind, firm, and well-focused. He let everyone do the work in his/her own way. He only cared for results. If the results were not there, he would review the process with the person concerned. He would work out, along with the employee, a new approach, and did the follow up all the way. It was a joy to work with him. They say good things don't last too long; he was diagnosed with a cancerous growth. He went off and on for treatment to Scotland, but continued with his normal rhythm of work when he was in office. My job was to design all the processes related to HR development, which included, orientation, career planning, training, and evaluation. I designed and developed all the above processes, and tested and implemented them, which took me two years. I was finally ready for retirement and went home for good. However, the company called me back to develop a Supervisor Manual on a contract basis, which took me six more months to complete. I finally retired with a lot of time in my hands and nothing to do. I never missed the early morning walk along the beach with Melody.

We travelled often to New Jersey to be with the children. Raising up children in a different country brings its own sets of joys and worries both for parents and children. Our children, having been born in Venezuela, became native speakers of Spanish, which eventually became the language spoken in the family. Subsequently they learned English and became good at it too. However, they spoke little of their parents' mother tongue, a South Indian language known as Malayalam. They had some knowledge of it by hearing us speak it. Several visits they had made to Kerala helped them refresh and build their vocabulary. They understood it better after every visit, but felt inhibited to speak it. Thus, they could not relate well with the uncles, aunts and cousins who lived in India. They spoke more and more Spanish and identified themselves more and more as Venezuelans and Latinos. Although they had some exposure to Indian people in Venezuela, their preferences were mostly influenced by the local culture in terms of food, dress, and social interactions. As they were growing up into adulthood, I brought up the discussion as to what their true identity was and what identity they would like to project into the future. This discussion was very important because their cultural foundations were examined which had many bearings on the choices they made and would make in the future. For example, the discussion as to whom they should marry was raised. After several sessions, the whole family came to the conclusion that their future partner should be a person who met the following three conditions: a university graduate, Catholic, and Indian or Latino or American. Also, an agreement was reached that they would begin dating only after graduating from the university. This was to assure that all their concentration was dedicated to their studies. All three of them respected this decision. However, in hind-sight, this limited their opportunity to find suitable partners early in life. It is at the high school and college level that most lasting relationships are established. Therefore, it took a while for our children to establish serious relationships.

Melody and I felt the time had come to say goodbye to Venezuela. We discussed with the children the idea of making the final move and they agreed with it. I went from New Jersey to Caracas to put the beach apartment on sale. Melody stayed behind. I got a real estate agent to help me out. Several people were interested, and one of them made an offer which was acceptable to us. But there was a condition: he had to sell his apartment in order to buy ours. He already had a buyer, and both sales had to be completed simultaneously. The signing of the option to buy/sell was fixed for a Monday for both the apartments in the public notary office. Melody was to arrive on Friday before, as she, too, had to sign the option. She took the flight from the New Jersey Newark Airport early in the morning to catch the flight from Miami to Caracas in the afternoon. But, at 9.00 AM on that day, the buyer of my apartment called me to let me know that he was unable to sign the option, as his own buyer had backed out. This came as a powerful bolt to my head. Melody was in the plane on her way to Miami. The only thing that occurred in my mind was to kneel down and pray. I prayed very hard for one hour, at the end of which I got another call from the buyer who let me know that he had arranged another buyer for his apartment and that the signing of the option would go as planned. I couldn't believe what I heard. My prayer had been answered so soon. It was very difficult in those days to get a buyer for an apartment. There were so many apartments on sale. To get a buyer in one hour's time was a miracle. If this was not a miracle, I didn't believe in any other miracles. Melody came, and the option was signed. The closing was set for the tenth of November, 2006.

Melody and I had to make the decision to sell or ship our belongings to India. We went around the shipping companies, asking for prices to wrap and send our belongings in a small container. We found out it was expensive, but decided to go forward with the idea anyway, as we both were attached emotionally to several things. If we had sold some of them in the market, we would not have gotten the money they were worth, as people would have expected us to sell cheap. The decision to take them along was a costly solution. We didn't have a better choice. Who has set price for emotions? Each of us finds happiness in our own head, and if this is the way we chose to be happy, so be it. Some may not agree with our choice of transporting the used things, instead of buying them new and cheaper in India. But who knows how much money we would have made by selling them in Venezuela? As we found out, the same things of equal quality were not available in India. The packers came and worked the whole day and took the boxes to the storage for shipment. That evening we moved into a hotel. The next day we went back to the apartment to clean up. We were invited by our friends in the building for a farewell party. Several people spoke of the loss of our departure. I spoke briefly of the thirty-four years we had spent in Venezuela and pointed out how we had enjoyed our stay, emphasizing the warmth and friendship that the people had bestowed on our family. Everyone present felt the pain of uprooting a tree that had grown up and spread roots far and wide. The next day we signed off the apartment and went to Caracas and checked into a hotel. There were several dinner invitations given by the Indian Association friends. As the plane left the Venezuelan shores, I looked back and vowed to be back someday. We spent a few days with the children in New Jersey, and took the flight to India to be there for the arrival of the ship. I slept off the route from Kuwait to Mumbai. When the plane touched down, I was woken up from a dream, wherein I was the last person in a march, with Gandhi at the head; he turned and looked at me as if he knew me. He beckoned me to go forward and join him.

We arrived home, this time with the decision to stay, although we had to return to the US to prepare for the wedding of our eldest daughter. But that was to be just a temporary absence. It took a while for the idea to sink into our head that we were going to stay and not just visiting. But the question always came up, where would we stay? We had to decide where we would settle down, what type of housing we would go for, whether we would rent or buy. These were not easy questions to answer. We went to the village of my ancestral home, where some of my brothers still live, but found it too hilly and without the minimum amenities that we are used to. We went to the place where Melody was born and raised, and found the place more inviting. We looked there for a place to buy. After searching for some time, we found a villa under construction. It was the last of the seven houses, which formed a gated community. Only the foundation was laid. We looked through the drawing and got an idea of it. We made the down payment right away. Melody was happy that she would live near her mother. I was a sporadic visitor to her hometown, all these years. This time I was going to be an immigrant. I had to get to know the pond I had chosen, and soon found myself venturing within its environment. I got used to it and made some friends. It was not that scary after all, to settle down in a new place. I had done it several times in my life. The shipment from Venezuela arrived, and we took things to storage. Soon, we had to leave for the US to get ready for Roshni's marriage. A thousand and one things had to be done before the event. It was our marriage, our arrangements, and our expenses. The marriage took place, and we patted our backs. Everybody enjoyed it, especially the food. Even after six years, people still remind us how much they enjoyed the feast. I consider it a miracle of God that I found myself in one piece after the event. Roshni and her husband left for Spain, and we left for India. The villa had advanced, but was still eight months away from occupation. We rented an apartment near and visited the villa every day. Finally, it was handed over as promised, and we moved into it with all our possessions. Our daughter Ranya came for the house warming. Our son also came four months later and liked the house. The next year we returned to NJ for the engagement of our son and waited for the arrival of our first granddaughter. While I was attending a marriage in Chicago, I was woken up in the middle of the night with the news that Roshni was in pains and had been taken to the hospital. I rushed to New Jersey and reached on time for the delivery. I did not want to be in the delivery room as I chickened out from seeing the pains through which my daughter had to go. Even after having pushed many times, the child would not come out. Ranya called me and asked me to go the chapel and pray to Jesus that He gives us a quick and safe delivery. I went into the chapel and prayed, "Jesus, please go with your mother and deliver the baby. I will take care of your chapel". Five minutes into my prayer, my son came and tapped my shoulder and told me that the baby had been born. It had been a normal delivery. I rushed to the room and found the baby girl in the arms of Melody. We had become happy grandparents. We called her Bibi, and now everybody calls her by that name. She was cute looking from the first day and continues to be so on her fourth birthday. She has never stopped surprising us with her talks, gestures, manners and dance movements. She has a sister now, two years-old, equally charming. She is the most tranquil and friendly child on earth. Everybody wants to carry her, and she obliges everyone. For the marriage of my son, we did not have to do much as the girl's party was in charge of it. Still, we had our traditions on the sides the previous day, which called for additional spending and arrangements. And then occurred the marriage of Ranya in Washington. It picked all my nerves. I came down with pneumonia and was in bed until one week before the event. Still, together with Ranya, we mustered all the energy to plan and carry-out all the activities that were required. Thank God, everything went as planned. We came back to India with all our energy drained. Still, one year into it, we were back in the US, this time to be present for the delivery of Ranya. The third granddaughter arrived two days after we reached. The merry-making continued. "To who has more, more will be given", says the Bible. And then the baptism of Roshni's second daughter happened, followed by the baptism of Ranya's daughter, a week later.

The next week, Melody and I went to Cancun, Mexico for vacations. Cancun is the place most visited by tourists in the world. It is located in the Yucatan peninsula, with the Gulf of Mexico to the north and the Atlantic Ocean to the east and south. The Yucatan Peninsula was ruled by the Mayas from 2000 BC to 900 AD. Mayas were the most developed people, the only culture with a written language in the Americas before the arrival of Christopher Columbus. They ruled a good part of Central America. They were known for architecture, mathematics, art, and religion. They developed a calendar that started 3013 years ago, which ended on the 21st of December 2012. Many ruins exist, including a Pyramid that we visited in Chechen Itza. There are still a lot Mayans in Mexico who try to carry on the traditions of the fore-fathers. After a week in Cancun, we flew to Mexico City, the capital of the country. An uncle of Melody who lives in the city picked us up. Cancun and Mexico City are show cases for tourists. There are lots of things to see in both places. Special mention has to be made of the following monuments that we visited in Mexico City: the sun and moon pyramids, the Church of the Virgin de Guadalupe, the Museum of Anthropology, the Fort of Chapultepec, and the National Cathedral, which is the biggest church in Latin America. A bus tour takes the tourists to all these places and many more. We left Mexico City very satisfied with our stay there. The uncle and his family contributed to making our stay very pleasant and productive.

The next day after we returned to the US, a granddaughter—the fourth one in the family—was born to our son. We did not have enough time to bond with her as we ran out of vacation time. It was high season, and we had to take the flight back. We reached home after very tiring flights. The house needed some caring. After getting over the jetlag, we settled down to our routines. Life is a constant restart of cycles. We are not making plans to return to the US in the near future. We have run our course.

Ever since, I came back to India, I have been meditating on the meaning of the dream I had on Gandhi as I was touching down at the Bombay Airport, five years ago. I have come to the conclusion that, if Gandhi was to be alive today, he would have launched another freedom struggle in India; a freedom struggle to liberate India from exploitation, corruption, child labor, illiteracy, violence, religious fanaticism, abuse of power, lack of service in public offices, poor education, discrimination, and bad politicians. Social consciousness and education are the most effective means of emancipation from the above illnesses. School education is weak in India. Of the hundred children that begin the first grade in the public schools in India, only fourteen pass high school (twelfth grade), and of these only four pass out of the university. The private schools have much better performance. The statistic varies with individual states. One can imagine the wastage that is produced by public education system. Imagine all the resources spent in the public sector only to graduate four percent of students from the university. Ninety-six percent are lost out on the way. Some of them are recycled into skills training in various areas and find careers as diploma holders. Many end up as auto rickshaw drivers. The reasons for the attrition in the school system are numerous. I have talked with many drop-outs of formal educational system. Their self esteem is very low as they feel that society considers them failures and losers. I want to set up a system to recuperate these drop-outs and potential dropouts. The latter group includes many disadvantaged in Indian society. I dream of a project to help them continue with their studies and complete a degree course in the university. I want to work with a few dropouts to help them learn not only technical skills, but also life, social, and personal skills to live a happy life. The model that I have in mind is the master-disciple relationship. I will take in a few students that have left their studies, or are about to leave, and work with them so that they complete a university degree. I will be their guru, and they will be my disciples. I will teach them or will make sure that they are taught all that they need to know to obtain a degree and lead an exemplary life.

The idea is to convert them into masters eventually so that they in turn can take students and form them into graduates. The cycle can continue indefinitely until all the dropouts throughout the world can be covered in the foreseeable future. If more masters can be recruited and trained, the process can be speeded up. I am sure it will have many problems during the phase of implementation, but with persistence and dedication, a lot of students can be formed into good and educated citizens, who can lead the country to a better future. I am sure Gandhi would have loved this project.